Praise for *Beyond Viral*

"The Internet democratized the world of entertainment—anyone can now instantly publish videos to the world. As a result, marketers face an intimidating number of options to reach their customers online. Never fear, Nalts is here. Kevin separates the wheat from the chaff, uncovering the best online opportunities for today's brands. Kevin has two things going for him: the experience to know what really works in the online video space, and the guts to share his secrets.

"Many content creators would give their right arm to make even one video that goes viral. Kevin Nalty has accomplished this feat over and over again. He either has a deal with the devil or he understands something most others don't. We are all truly lucky he is willing to teach us so much of what he has learned. His knowledge and his frankness will astonish you.

"Professional TV content seems to attract most of the attention from marketers these days. Fortunately, Kevin knows one of the Internet's best kept secrets: there is enormous marketing power in the videos produced by a new generation of storytellers. Call them You Tube stars, web-lebrities, or something else, these amateur video creators reach audiences that would make TV's biggest producers green with envy. Kevin explains how to work with them, save money doing it, and monitor your success along the way."

—Joe Michaels, Senior Director MSN and Bing, Microsoft Corporation

"Kevin Nalty is and has been my go-to guy on all things viral video, and now he is sharing his expertise with the world. Years of being a marketer by day and 'Viral Video Genius' by night make him one of only a few people truly qualified to write such a book. You'll learn, laugh, and learn some more as 'Nalts' shares his experience and unique expertise in a fun yet very informative way."

—Michael Donnelly
Group Director, Worldwide Interactive Marketing
The Coca-Cola Company

"Nalts is a gentleman, a scholar, and a lunatic. Read his book and then destroy it immediately."

—Tom Green
Comedian, Actor, and Host of TomGreen.com

"In this must-read for marketers—and for those simply interested in learning more about the evolving world of video and social media—Kevin provides ample insight that will prove more than worth the weight of this book in Unobtainium. The world has seen many faces of Nalty: brand marketing professional, YouTube master, and now the author. We find ourselves delighted, intrigued, and ultimately better informed by the talents of his unique creative mind."

—Del Ross
Vice President, U.S. Sales & Marketing
InterContinental Hotels Group (Holiday Inn, Crowne Plaza)

"Kevin is one of the few people who actually 'gets' viral video. As a career marketer for companies including Johnson & Johnson, he understands what businesses need from their online video marketing, as well as the opportunities, risks, and pitfalls that must be carefully navigated in this space. As one of the most successful video creators on YouTube, he also understands what generates results in online video. You won't just learn about online video, you'll learn how to make it work for your business—real world instruction from someone who does this every day. And who makes great fart videos."

—Brad Aronson
Author, Advertising on the Internet
Fmr. Executive Vice President, Product Development, aQuantative
and Senior Director Advertiser and Publisher
Solutions, Microsoft

BEYOND VIRAL

HOW TO ATTRACT CUSTOMERS, PROMOTE YOUR BRAND, AND MAKE MONEY WITH ONLINE VIDEO

KEVIN H. NALTY

WILEY

John Wiley & Sons, Inc.

This book is dedicated to the memory of my father,
Paul A. Nalty, who taught me to live for God and others,
and whose death in July 2009 was one of those great
losses that brings deeper meaning to life.

Contents

Foreword by David Meerman Scott   *ix*

Acknowledgments   *xii*

About the Author   *xiii*

Introduction   *xiv*

Chapter 1   **The Least a Marketer Needs to Know**   **1**

Chapter 2   **Flavors of Video: From Skateboarding Cats to Pro**   **31**

Chapter 3   **Viral Video Is Dead**   **43**

Chapter 4   **Video's Role in the Marketing Funnel**   **59**

Chapter 5   **The Most Visceral Form of Social Media**   **79**

Chapter 6   **Inside YouTube**   **91**

Chapter 7   **Agencies Searching for Role**   **105**

Chapter 8   **Learning from Online-Video "Stars"**   **121**

Chapter 9   **Marketing via Webstars**   **131**

Chapter 10 **Paid Video Advertising**   **145**

Chapter 11 **Measuring ROI and Performance of Online Video**   **155**

Chapter 12 Video and Search Engine Optimization 163

Chapter 13 How to Get Popular on YouTube 177

Chapter 14 Can You Make Money from 205
　　　　　　Online Video?

Chapter 15 Guerrilla Video for Entrepreneurs and 217
　　　　　　Cause-Related Marketing

Chapter 16 Learning from Obama Girl by 225
　　　　　　Ben Relles

Chapter 17 Insider Information: Behind 233
　　　　　　the Curtain

Chapter 18 The Future of Online Video 261

Notes 267

Index 273

Foreword

I just annoyed my family. Again.

I was laughing uncontrollably, watching one of Kevin Nalty's videos. This has become a common occurrence around my house. My wife and daughter just roll their eyes and treat me like an 80-year-old deranged uncle drooling in the corner when I get this way. This time the culprit was his brilliant "Mall Pranks," which has been watched 6.5 million times on YouTube. Then I start cracking up again, because "Mall Pranks" features Kevin's wife, and all I can think of is how lucky she is to live with Kevin because he's so entertaining. But wait, ... Maybe it would suck to live with Kevin because he's kind of annoying, too. Hmm . . .

But I'm getting ahead of myself.

A while ago, I was interviewed by the *Wall Street Journal* for an article (and companion video) about how small businesses can leverage online video. Kevin challenged some of the observations by the *WSJ* reporter Raymund Flandez on his WillVideoForFood.com site.

I immediately hightailed it over to Kevin's video channels to see who he was. I was awestruck. Here was a guy who could generate more YouTube views in the time it takes to walk around the block than I had amassed in my entire life. So I knew I needed to take his points seriously. But then I realized something remarkable. Kevin was about much more than just doing silly videos like his "Farting in Public" (now seen more than 10 million times on YouTube alone). I learned Kevin is actually a career marketer who has held senior roles in some of the world's largest corporations!

So I commented on his blog and we began a personal relationship that led directly to this book.

Last year Kevin left his job as marketing director at Merck & Company. Perhaps, like my forced departure from The Thompson Corporation seven years earlier, this was a result of his being too radical for his bosses.

In the past year he has been consulting with brands on video, social media, and innovation. He speaks at conferences, advises corporations, and has written extensively about this rapidly evolving online-video space. His perspective as both a YouTube celebrity and a marketing professional gives him a unique perspective on what works and what doesn't in the uncharted waters of viral videos. I knew Kevin would be the best person on the planet to write a book about using video to attract customers, promote brands, and make money. I am thrilled he agreed to write this book.

Whether you're a CEO, a marketer, an agency leader, or an entrepreneur, *Beyond Viral* will provide actionable ideas and plans that can save you from many pitfalls and help you market successfully via online video. Consider it four years of intensive practice—as a marketer and an entertainer—packed into one book.

In fact when I sat down with the manuscript, I read it in one sitting.

I laughed. *A lot*.

But I learned a lot, too.

Don't expect this to read like your typical business book. *Beyond Viral* is written by a guy who manages to be taken seriously by major corporate clients . . . when he's not secretly videotaping people's reactions to him crawling through airports, pratfalling in the snow, or having fake panic attacks in New York City cabs.

—David Meerman Scott
Businessweek best-selling author of
The New Rules of Marketing & PR
www.WebInkNow.com
twitter.com/dmscott

Acknowledgments

Thank you to my wife, Jo Lewis Nalty, who has stood patiently by me despite all my idiosyncrasies. I am also profoundly grateful to my four beautiful children (Katie, Patrick, Grant, and Charlie), who permit me to share their childhood with the world via online video. One day they may thank me for enabling perpetual, real-time access to happy and bizarre memories of their youth. More likely, as my siblings caution, they will repay me in my later years by rolling my wheelchair down steps and posting the footage on the Internet. However, my family is a constant reminder to dwell neither on the past nor future, but in the joyful experience of the present.

I also deeply appreciate the wisdom and guidance of Brad Aronson, David Meerman Scott, Steve Garfield, and the people at John Wiley & Sons. Thank you also to the many people who helped along the way, including Mathilde Mellon, Eric Vandal, Nicholas Guillen, and Jan Ischinger. Without them you would not be holding this book, and I would be in my fifth year of procrastination.

Finally, a special thank you to those of you who watch my videos—especially those who have been watching from the beginning and continue to encourage me, or at least tolerate me.

About the Author

Kevin H. Nalty is the only career marketer who is one of the most-viewed online-video personalities, and his thousands of videos have been seen several hundred million times online. Known on YouTube as "Nalts," his videos have appeared on nearly every major television network, have been featured on leading video-sharing sites, and were honored by the Webby Awards. Nalty speaks internationally at corporations and conferences, was named a 2010 *Streaming Media* magazine "All Star," and has covered the evolution of online video since 2006 via his blog, WillVideoForFood.com. He has led innovation at Johnson & Johnson, was a product director at Merck and Co., Inc., and has worked at interactive agencies and with Big Five consulting. He received his B.A. from Georgetown University and his MBA from Babson College. Today he leads Nalts Consulting, helping companies and brands engage with customers via the most visceral form of social media: online video.

Introduction

A great author, especially a marketer, would spare no words before telling you why this book is so vital to you. Alas, I'm not a great author. Unlike those behind the other books adorning your shelves, I am perhaps more like you. What I lack in raw talent I make up for in voracious curiosity and persistence. I don't exercise or floss daily, but I thrive on disruptive change and have a passion for lifelong learning.

I have written this book because I feel that *most books about online video have missed the mark*. I'll offer four theories: (1) The medium is changing so rapidly that none of us understand it entirely; (2) the majority of YouTube books are simply dull how-to instructions; (3) many books focus on video production and not business implications; and (4) some are written by writers. We have already established that I am not a writer, and if you decide otherwise, the editors deserve credit. I am a career marketer, a dad, a video enthusiast, and someone who happens to have fooled millions of online-video viewers into thinking I am a celebrity.

Online video offers profound opportunities for people and businesses, and I hope this book can be your shortcut to seizing them. As both a career marketer and online-video creator, I have participated actively in this new medium since 2005 (the year YouTube launched). I have watched, studied, and analyzed this ecosystem somewhat compulsively, as my family might observe. I regularly speak at industry conferences, educate marketers, and write about it via my blog (WillVideoForFood.com) and in trade

Figure I.1 A YouTube documentary, "I Want My Three Minutes Back," chronicles the author's misadventures, seen here with his 14-year-old prankster, Spencer.

publications. My journey, which was chronicled in a documentary titled "I Want My Three Minutes Back," is something I hope can save you time (Figure I.1). I also have engaged in online video as a full-time marketing director at Johnson & Johnson and Merck, and with such clients as Coke, Microsoft, General Electric, Fox Broadcasting, Starbucks, Holiday Inn, Mentos, and MTV.

I tell you this not just to brag, but to let you know you are holding a compressed file representing thousands of hours of research and experience. Unzip it to save yourself time, catch up, avoid pitfalls, and zoom past competitors. Or read it cover-to-cover if you feel so inclined. But please at least read the first chapters, and then dive into practical insights that can specifically help you in your business, artistic, volunteer, or other pursuits.

In addition to setting your expectations about my writing, I need to make two additional disclaimers. First, I am not the brightest marketer (although at least I am enlightened to that fact). Second, I am far from the most talented or popular online-video creator. I am, however, the only career marketer today who is also one of the most-viewed personalities on YouTube. My more than 1,000 videos have been seen hundreds of millions of times. They're lowbrow humor—Doritos™ for the brain, if you will. But surprisingly, more people watch them each day than some of the television shows you know well. My videos range from sophomoric candid-camera-style pranks to heartfelt family moments. My mom takes little pride in knowing they can find my opus video ("Farting in Public") by simply searching Google for the word *fart*. (See Figure I.2.)

Lest you think my YouTube fame has gone to my head, let me be clear it does not carry many special privileges or bring me great fortune. I playfully call myself a *viral video genius*,

Figure I.2 YouTube is the second-most popular search engine after Google. A Google search of the word "Fart" reveals the author's "Farting in Public" video on YouTube.

or *weblebrity*. Of course, I have only been recognized in public a total of three times (each time more thrilling to me than the viewer). My 15 minutes of fame has lasted longer than I might have anticipated, however; it has allowed me to meet some real-life stars, and that's been a real treat. But you won't see me on red carpets or at the Hollywood parties. My income as a YouTube Partner, while not trivial, is not enough to substantiate a family of six.

I make comedic-like videos. I can't call my videos *comedy* any more than Kraft™ can refer to its "cheese products" as actual cheese. Fortunately, my wife and family have tolerated this hobby because it does create nontrivial income. More important, studying and practicing online video is what I would be doing even if I won the lottery. I am combining two of my strongest passions (besides family, of course): marketing and online video.

There is great irony in my writing a book that includes *viral* in the title. Viral is a term that originated to refer to a biological agent (an infectious agent that can replicate inside the cells of other organisms). It was later used to refer to computer programs (usually harmful) that could infect a computer through reproductive processes. Marketers in the mid-1990s borrowed the term to describe marketing and advertising that would *go viral* via word-of-mouth or through preexisting social mediums. As videos became easier to share via e-mail and online-video web sites in the late 1990s, certain video clips became widely circulated, and the term *viral video* was born.

Leave it to us marketers, who refer to customers as "targets," to turn an infectious agent into a noble pursuit. Most viral videos are funny or bizarre clips created by individuals. One of the first examples of a viral video featured a crude webcam video by Gary Brolsma, a New Jersey teenager.

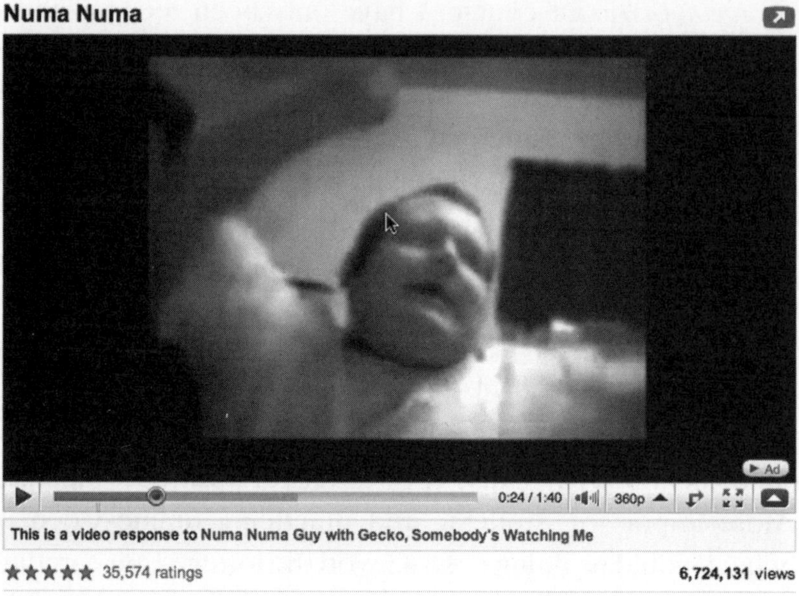

Numa Numa

This is a video response to Numa Numa Guy with Gecko, Somebody's Watching Me

★★★★★ 35,574 ratings   6,724,131 views

Figure I.3   "Numa Numa" boy takes the stage.

Brolsma lip-synched to a song called "Dragostea Din Tei" by a Romanian band O-Zone, which contained the refrain "Numa Numa." He submitted the clip to Newgrounds.com in December 2004, and it was widely circulated and featured on many popular television shows.[1] (See Figure I.3.)

One of my first viral videos was, in fact, a mockery of viral. In a self-deprecating video called "Viral Video Genius," I parodied the pomposity of celebrated artists as if going viral actually mattered. (See Figure I.4.) I have since proclaimed viral dead, at least for advertisers. I should add that being viewed millions of times is a bit less satisfying than you might expect.

When I speak, I often beg marketers to go beyond the roulette game of a viral advertisement, since there are many smarter ways to tap online video to reach target customers and drive sales. If you picked up this book hoping to go

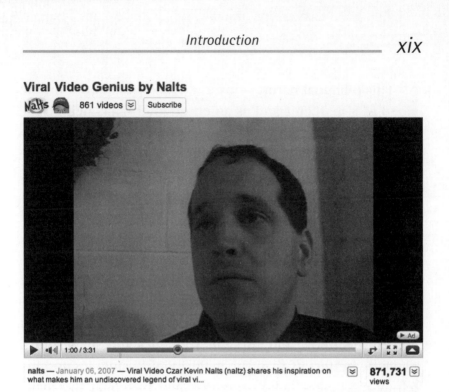

Viral Video Genius by Nalts

Nalts 861 videos ⊻ Subscribe

1:00 / 3:31 ▶ Ad

nalts — January 06, 2007 — Viral Video Czar Kevin Nalts (naltz) shares his inspiration on what makes him an undiscovered legend of viral vi... ⊻ **871,731** ⊻ views

Figure I.4 "The Author's "Viral Video Genius" spoofs a documentary interview of a self-important artist boasting of his viral-video success. When it was featured on YouTube's home page in 2007, those not watching the complete video took it seriously.

viral, I hope to walk you down a road less traveled, where the grass is most definitely greener.

My passion, combined with my unique role as a hybrid career marketer and weblebrity, gives me a unique peek into how small companies and large brands can engage successfully in online video. Certainly, my marketing skills have given me an edge over more talented video creators (and to appease my guilty conscience, I once published a free e-book called *How to Become Popular on YouTube Without Any Talent*). I lost money on each copy, but made it up in volume when TechCrunch, a group-edited blog about technology start-ups, featured it.[2]

This bilingual nature—my ability to speak about online video as a marketer and as an entertainer—has helped my employers and clients. But for years, I have wanted to more broadly influence the online-video strategy and tactics pursued by businesses, marketers, advertisers, studios, and agencies. Last year, I resigned as a product director at Merck and Co., Inc., in what Cracked.com called one of the "ballsiest" resignations ever.[3] Before working at Merck, I was a leader at Johnson & Johnson, interactive agencies, and Big Five consulting. Now, I am merging my passions via Nalts Consulting (www.NaltsConsulting.com).

That's enough about me (at least for now). If you can absorb this book, and apply its strategies and suggestions, you'll be better off than the majority of businesses and my fellow marketers, who seem doomed to repeat the many failed attempts of others in this medium. I wish I could upload my experience in its entirety for instant download. Since that is not yet possible, I have done my best to distill what I've learned the hard way, and give you useful tips to engage your target audience, market your business or service, and increase sales. If you do, please let me know. My e-mail is kevinnalty@gmail.com, and I would be thrilled to learn how this book helped you.

CHAPTER 1

The Least a Marketer Needs to Know

In this chapter, you will learn:

- Why a marketer needs to know about online video.

- Pitfalls to avoid and ways to save yourself time and money.

- How to target customers in ways you may not have considered.

- How video can help you from awareness through loyalty.

Presumably, you would not be reading these words if you had not recognized that online video can help drive businesses. However, I feel compelled to point out why I think this is the most interesting thing happening in our time:

- Online video generally refers to viewing that occurs at a computer, and that remains the prevailing mode today. Over time, however, the convergence of the *three screens* (television, computer, and mobile devices) will further complicate the definition of *online video* and perhaps eventually make the term antiquated and obsolete.

- This medium is disrupting industries and traditional networks, and content producers have so far fumbled and lost relevancy in online video. While most video viewing is done via a television set, the audience has continued to fragment. In the early 1950s, more than 30 percent of households watched NBC, and today it's around 5 percent.[1] As television audiences fragment and shift to online viewing, marketing dollars are following them.

- Today, online video is the only advertising medium with a growth rate estimated at 40 to 60 percent per year,[2] while such traditional areas of marketing mix as television and print are flat or declining.[3] (See Figure 1.1.)

- YouTube remains the dominant player in online video, so this book gives it disproportionate attention. By the time you read this book, we'll likely see a reduction of the approximately 37 percent share difference between the leading video property and its distant follower. ComScore, a market research company that tracks one of the largest panels of online users, reports that Google/YouTube leads with nearly 40 percent share, followed by Hulu with only 3 percent.[4] Still, approximately 25 percent of Google search queries are conducted on YouTube, making it the number two search engine (above Yahoo!).[5] YouTube also has more content and active viewers than any television network.

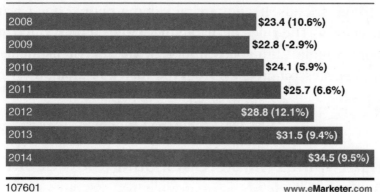

Figure 1.1   U.S. online advertising spending, 2008–2014 (billions and % change).

Source: eMarketer, October 2009.

Online video—like radio, television, and film—has created a new type of star. Individual "one-man band" amateurs are being watched more frequently than most television shows. Brands have a near-term opportunity to partner with these stars for cost-efficient ways of reaching large audiences. Many of these individuals are earning six-figure annual incomes via advertisers.

Online video is changing the way we market, and requires insights they don't teach in business school (at least they didn't a decade ago, but now I'm dating myself). On the one hand, we have marketers believing their unique selling proposition is as interesting as the "Numa Numa" kid.[6]

On the other hand, we have today's attention-deficit video viewers (which I will explain in depth later) demanding hyperpaced video entertainment, and ready to skip or close a video otherwise. So the rules of creating videos are fairly simple: Keep your clip or video short, interesting, edgy, and give us a surprise that makes us want to forward it to our friends. It's not a viral video if people don't want to share it. The rules of marketing within online video are more complex, but you will soon be capable of distinguishing a successful program from the road kills along the viral highway.

Eight Things Marketers Should Know about Online Video

I like lists, so allow me start with an important one. There are eight things every marketer should know about online video. To fully understand these, it has taken me several years of experimenting as a marketer and video creator. You, however, will learn much more quickly. Read these closely and you will save months of frustration, reduce your costs and risks, impress your colleagues, and possibly even lose 20 pounds in two weeks.

1. They're Watching. Your customers are watching exponentially more videos online than they were even a year ago. A marketer cannot survive without some skepticism, but trust me on this one. The early adopters of online video (technical enthusiasts, teenagers, video gamers) are giving way to a broader audience that will, eventually, closely represent the population. Americans continue to spend as much as 10 times more time in front of their televisions than surfing the Internet or watching online video. But three trends are capturing the attention of advertisers: (1) Time-shifted television viewing is increasing rapidly (with the proliferation of digital video recorders), (2) there is a significant (35 percent) rise in simultaneous use of the television and Internet, and (3) online-video viewing is increasing rapidly across all demographics.[7]

2. Your Brand Isn't an Online-Video Entertainer. It is a rare marketer or brand that can also entertain. It is the role of a marketer to identify a target market with a need, position a product or service into the minds of its customers, and grow sales. Those tasks often are at odds with the job of an entertainer, which is to engage and delight audiences. I happen to wear both hats, and it is challenging to balance these roles. Many marketers, often with help from creative agencies, have created "branded entertainment" flops like the now-defunct Bud.tv, the first attempt by a consumer product company to launch a full-scale TV network with original long-form programming online.[8] (See Figure 1.2.)

Budweiser makes beer, and would have been better served by introducing its products in the context of popular existing shows and audiences. Assume, even if you believe otherwise, that nobody cares about your brand but you. Find content that already attracts crowds, and develop creative ways of working with the creators and distributors. Instead

Figure 1.2 All that remains of Bud.tv.

of trying to launch a Broadway show about your product, slip down the street into a standing-room-only theater. You would be surprised how receptive the creators can be.

3. It's a Buyer's Market. The ROI (return on investment) of reaching customers via online video is surprisingly high; like most new mediums, it is a buyer's market. There are plenty of eyeballs with wallets, and an abundance of made-for-Web video content. Yet advertising dollars have not yet adjusted. In many ways, online video is like what search engine marketing was in 2000. Too many companies are stuck in a repetitive "ready, aim" mode, and only a few industries (entertainment, travel, and consumer packaged goods) are beginning to harness the power of online video. If you spend the next six months making the first step, you may lose opportunities, and also likely discover that the medium has changed again.

4. You'll Need a Sherpa. A calculated investment in online video means: (1) being prudent about spending, (2) respecting the rules of social media, (3) engaging audiences in interesting ways, and (4) analyzing results carefully. Many brands awkwardly apply the interruption-advertising model from television and online marketing.

The best way to be prudent and stay within social media is to find a sherpa who has learned the trails of the mountain. Most of them, myself included, will be annoying. Just as social-media gurus are sprouting like dandelions, everyone claims to be an online-video expert. But there are individuals who have achieved success, have made mistakes along the way, and know where the land mines are hiding. The best way to know how someone will approach online video is to understand what he or she did previously. You'll get different perspectives, depending on if someone came from marketing, advertising, creative, online, production, television, or film (or last year happened to be a guru of SecondLife.com, a once popular virtual world).

5. ROI Soup. Every list has a "measure-and-improve" step, but let's get specific. Very few brands can truly measure the direct impact on sales of online video, and that makes it surprisingly consistent with the rest of the marketing mix. Still, it is not hard to cook up an ROI soup made of behavioral data, test-control research, and educated assumptions. Even better, the targeting and metrics—provided marketers and advertisers demand it—are getting almost as good as paid search, and certainly much better than print or television. As a product director I doubled my paid-search budgets nearly every year, despite not having a precise indicator of resulting sales. I used a solid assumption-based ROI model, and it impressed me more than television, radio, print GRPs (gross rating points), and studies on consumer awareness and attitudes. If you can't track sales directly to online video, you can at least ensure you are not budget bleeding by doing a simple test-control or pre-post study using the proxy measures or drivers of sales (enrollment, site visit, intent, awareness).

6. An Impression Isn't an Impression unless It Makes One. Television is still bought based on gross rating points, and online advertising is purchased by cost per impression (CPM). In another life, I must have been a direct-response junkie because that makes me very sad. Views or impressions can be horribly deceptive. They can give a brand the false pride of going viral with no sales consequence. A well-targeted video could be inadvertently scorned because it was seen only 100,000 times—but these viewers could be the target buyers. The question is not "how many views?" but whether a target saw it and changed his or her behavior. Most online marketers know that the vast majority of banner ads are not even seen (based on eye-tracker studies). Videos, by contrast, tend to engage a person actively—even if it is just for a minute or less. What we marketers really want is behavior change, and that happens when prospects give us time, attention, and engagement. But the CPM ad model tells us little about those vital signs. We want reach, but we need engagement to lift intent to purchase or generate sales. Just as a piece of junk mail can't do the job of a good salesperson, a cheap display advertisement can't perform like online video (and even those adjacent ads, to a lesser degree). I believe online video is the most visceral, engaging, and persuasive form of mass entertainment and marketing. This is amplified when there's already a bond between the person in the video and her audience.

7. Please Don't Just Advertise. Every marketer will eventually use online video to advertise. But I hope you will think beyond traditional ad buys—online video is a vehicle with potential to go much farther. It has implications on social media, public relations, communication, and education. Display advertising has merits, but a brand can often have greater impact with content sponsorships, product placement, and relationships with video creators and distributors. Even individual video stars are like mini-networks or publications of their own. They have loyal audiences, and you want your marketing to do more than interrupt the relationship between them and their audience. This industry is still young enough for you to be the online-video equivalent of a marketer who had E.T. holding Reese's Pieces, provided Oprah with her first free audience give-aways, or placed the Coke cup in the hands of the judges on *American Idol*.

8. Understand the Ecosystem. Online video has turned amateurs into stars, web sites into networks, and

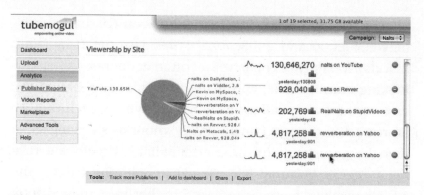

Figure 1.3 TubeMogul, founded in 2006 by graduate students at UC Berkeley, helps producers distribute video to dozens of video-sharing sites and track performance.

interactive agencies into entertainers. It has also created a number of successful new entrants and far more defunct intermediaries. As the marketplace matures, it will sort itself out. Eventually, people and companies will return to their core competencies, but prepare for at least a decade of rapid-fire evolution. Right now, the least you need to know is that there are creators, distributors, destination sites, Web studios, creative agencies, individual video stars, and some specialty intermediaries that help link stars to brands (Hitviews, PlaceVine, and Poptent), or help video creators upload to multiple video-sharing sites and measure results (TubeMogul.com). (See Figure 1.3.)

Evolution of Online-Video Marketing

You may already have made up your mind about online video if you are familiar with the viral clichés: sneezing pandas, hissing cat, a fat guy smashing a computer, and the 1970s news story about exploding the beached whale. But you'll gain some additional perspective if we can take a quick journey back to the ancient days of online video.

1. Viral. Following YouTube's 2005 launch, in the years between 2006 and 2008, *viral video* was the Holy Grail. Brands invested in expensive and often deliberately amateur-looking commercials, and many had great success. In the case of the Dove Evolution campaign, which attempted to lift the self-esteem of females everywhere by showing them that they are beautiful no matter what, as well as a relatively recent Evian ad featuring skateboarding babies, the ads themselves were so remarkable that they indeed took on a life of their own. People forwarded them on to friends, so on and so forth, and they became most-viewed videos, where they found a secondary audience. Unfortunately, this is roulette marketing, as exponentially more viral commercials fail than succeed. To abuse my least-favorite marketing metaphor: *There are lower-hanging fruit.*

2. Seeding. Many videos gain appeal when they're *seeded* by agencies to social networks like Digg, Twitter, and Facebook. Seeding is the act of promoting your video to bloggers and via social-network sites. The most targeted views are those that occur on the web sites and blogs where your customers live. For example, a video promotion of a hotel or airline may get fewer views on travel-related web sites, but those are more valuable to the brand than views of my videos on YouTube.

3. Pay-per-View. In the delightful early days of online video, a small "under-the-table" media budget could, indeed, prime a video via covert home-page love on some second-tier sites. Even a home-page advertisement on YouTube would generate millions of views, although many of these views were simply "curiosity clicks" from people not realizing it was an ad. Today's YouTube home-page advertisements draw fewer views than in years prior, as the audience has become more savvy. So, YouTube has identified other ways to drive promotional views: It mixes popular online video as promotional content in what it calls spotlight videos. It has also invited advertisers to create explosive takeovers on its home page, which I always find odd coming from the folks who brought you Google. Many smaller online-video sites offer "paid view" guarantees ranging from 5 cents to a dollar per view ($5 to $1,000 CPM). Unfortunately, the viewers do not stay long when they realize the video is merely overt promotion, unless, of course, it is entertaining, engaging, or extremely relevant. Furthermore, many brands and agencies sink $100,000 to $500,000 into the production of authentic-looking viral videos, making the ROI nearly impossible unless it goes viral. If your agency refers to a video idea as viral, remind them it's actually a misnomer to call an online video viral unless it actually *goes viral*.

4. Ads Surrounding Videos. Because viewers of online video are engaged in the content (or they would disengage before an advertisement is shown), the online ads appearing before, during, or adjacent to videos tend to be more productive than banners on static content (see Figure 1.4 for various YouTube advertising format specifications). Most online-video advertising estimates refer only to this type of promotion (and not sponsored content or branded entertainment, as that spending is harder to capture). Those

Ad Type	Unit	File Types	Max File Size: Flash	Max File Size: JPG/GIF	Max Animation	Audio
Skyscraper	160 x 600	SWF/JPG/GIF	50KB	30KB	15 seconds	No
Large Rec	300 x 250	SWF/JPG/GIF	50KB	30KB	15 seconds	No
Titlecard	300 x 225	JPG	N/A	20KB	N/A	No
Small Rec	300 x 35	SWF/JPG/GIF	30KB	20KB	15 seconds	No
InVideo Overlay*	480 x 70	SWF AND FLA	100KB	N/A	10 seconds	No

Figure 1.4 YouTube advertisement formats: Just one part of a comprehensive online video strategy.

pop-up advertisements that appear in the bottom portion of a YouTube video are called InVideo ads, and they are more expensive because they are harder to ignore. Since these premium ads command more attention, they should drive more awareness, intent, and purchase than the "bargain-basement" banner buys across ad networks.

Have you ever noticed that every ad network insists on calling itself a *premium* ad network? Ads surrounding video work well for brands that do not have video content, or those that need broad and immediate reach. As viewers become savvier or more sensitized, the interaction rates will only decline. While my income depends on these pop-up ads, I've noticed that even my children instinctively close them. They are annoying. YouTube and other online-video sites, of course, will develop more creative and effective ways to engage prospects while they are enjoying videos.

Recent research by Nielsen IAG and Microsoft compared online-video ads and television commercials. Online performed better on a variety of measures, most likely because of increased engagement, inability to skip the ad, and less clutter. Recall was 65 percent for online and 46 percent for TV, while likability was 26 percent online and 14 percent on TV.[9] Additional research by *Advertising Age* showed that some video ads can increase awareness by 37.8 percent,[10] but that obviously depends highly on the creativity and the context. My simple litmus test: The ad succeeds if it would be difficult for someone to describe the advertisement without mentioning the brand.

5. Webstars. The most frequently viewed online-video stars are talented individuals with a collective audience that surpasses many television shows in daily viewership. We call them "webstars," "YouTube Stars," and "weblebrities." Like the first stars of television and radio, they have loyal audiences among both early adopters and the increasing mainstream audience watching exponentially more videos online than even a year ago. Unlike film and television stars, however, they have personal relationships with their audiences, and their audiences follow them across dozens of online-video sites, their own web sites, blogs, and social-media services (from Twitter to Facebook). To illustrate the impact of these stars, consider that the top 100 YouTube Partner channels represent the vast majority of revenue for YouTube, which monetizes the videos in a variety of ways (see Figure 1.5 for an example of most-subscribed YouTube Partners). Perhaps 95 percent of YouTube views are of content that is consumer-generated. They are not easily monetized. YouTube's primary income, aside from its *home-page takeover*, is driven by a relatively small number of individuals and corporations within YouTube Partner accounts.

While many of these Partner channels are those of musicians or professional content creators like Discovery Channel or BBC, the majority are made up of the aforementioned webstars.

6. Branded Entertainment. In truth, branded entertainment predates the Internet, but it remains all the rage. Hollywood wants corporations to invest in production, and then to market it with advertising dollars. Just like Procter & Gamble invented the soap opera to reach stay-at-home moms, some brilliant marketer is going to partner with a Hollywood studio to create a dazzlingly rich media experience that sells product. Do I sound skeptical? I am. More on that later.

7. Professional Content. For three years, I have predicted that the dominance of amateur weblebrities would soon fade behind more seasoned video creators. I've been

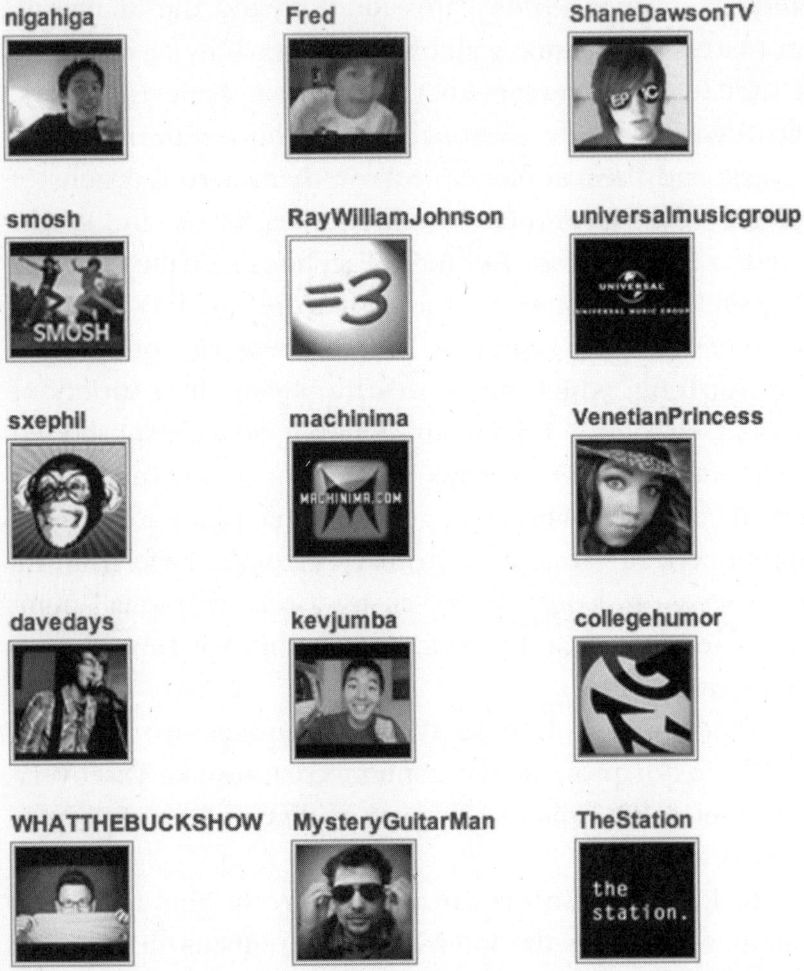
nigahiga
Fred
ShaneDawsonTV
smosh
SMOSH
RayWilliamJohnson
=3
universalmusicgroup
UNIVERSAL
sxephil
machinima
MACHINIMA.COM
VenetianPrincess
davedays
kevjumba
collegehumor
WHATTHEBUCKSHOW
MysteryGuitarMan
TheStation
the
station.

Figure 1.5 Most-viewed YouTube channels are often professionals, but the most-subscribed list is dominated by webstars.

prematurely predicting the demise of my species, as the amateur video star still dominates the most-viewed and most-subscribed videos. In the coming years, I would expect to see professional video content increase viewership online, but as a marketer I'm not interested in subsidizing it. A network, video site, or content providers should be aggregating an audience, and then turning to marketers for advertising. I am perplexed by brands that feel compelled to subsidize video content and promote it using their marketing budget. While there are attractive opportunities to achieve evolved relationship between brands, distributors, and content providers, a marketer's budget is not designed to promote content alone.

8. Video for Business throughout Customer Funnel. Increasingly, businesses are recognizing that viral video to drive awareness is only one application of the medium. Businesses are using video content to drive customer acquisition, educate, and improve customer relations. This will be explored in depth in Chapter 4, "Video's Role in the Marketing Funnel."

Online-Video Growth

By Daisy Whitney

"Video ad spending growth will far outpace any other online format, running in the 34 to 45 percent range from 2009 through 2014," said David Hallerman, an eMarketer senior analyst. "These extremely high growth rates are the result of video ads moving from the sidelines to center stage, becoming the main form of brand advertising in the digital space."

Marketers like video advertising because it's more effective and it's also familiar to them. They can also easily shift budgets and creatives onto the Web.

In addition, video delivers a return on investment. Brands using online video ads have seen lifts of anywhere from 20 to 40 percent or higher in terms of incremental

(Continued)

buying with online video and rich media over other ad forms, as comScore CEO Gian Fulgoni has said. ComScore tracks the impact of online video ads by measuring whether Internet users who saw an online video ad then went on to visit a site or buy a product, for instance.

In fact, for these reasons eMarketer projects video will grow to command more than $5 billion in ad spend in 2014, up from $1 billion last year. That number will put video as one of the top three categories online, behind online banner ads and search ads. By 2014, search ads will corral about $16 billion in ad spend, while banner ads will generate about $6 billion.

But in the near term, don't expect major advances in video formats online. Pre-rolls will continue to dominate on the Web. According to online video ad network YuMe, about 95 percent of the ads YuMe (and most other video networks) serve are of the pre-roll format.

That's because most advertisers prefer cutting down existing TV commercials for the Web into 15- and 30-second pre-rolls and they'll likely continue on that path in 2010.

But there is a growing body of evidence that advertisers can generate a higher return on investment when they create tailored ads, often using a pre-roll as the springboard.

Both YuMe and competitive online video ad network ScanScout have found that engagement rates with video ads are three to four times higher when a marketer uses custom spots, creative, and interactivity than they are for simple pre-roll ads.

YuMe served up more than 3 billion video ads in the first nine months of 2009 and found that when advertisers customize the creative for the online video medium they can garner as high as a 5 percent clickthrough rate, or engagement rate. (The average customized spot generates double the interaction of pre-rolls, which clock in at about 1 percent interaction, YuMe found.) Some of the clients for whom YuMe has served up tailored ads include Axe, Dove, Vitamin Water, Universal Pictures, and Land Rover.

"We see up to 5 percent click yields when people really take the time to develop creative that is online-specific and have the opportunity to engage the audience versus taking a TV ad and sticking it in front of the content," said Michael Mathieu, CEO of YuMe.

Because of the success with tailored ads, YuMe is exploring additional types of online video ad formats such as embedding ad units in the video. That could include contextually relevant ads layered on top of the video itself, Mathieu shared.

Competitive video ad network ScanScout has also found that customized spots yield much higher engagement rates. Interactive ads that let customers participate in polls, for instance, are generating four times better clickthrough rates than standard pre-rolls, said ScanScout, citing data from a recent Vaseline campaign run across its network.

The Vaseline campaign included a pre-roll unit that allowed users to vote on their favorite features of the lotion. Interactivity can also include letting viewers opt in to receive coupons or more information on a product.

(Continued)

As advertisers shift more dollars to the Web and as more studies pointing to the effectiveness of interactivity and customization emerge, marketers are apt to experiment with those video formats as well as placing bets on tried-and-true pre-rolls, experts say.

Figure 1.6   Daisy Whitney is a producer and on-air correspondent, and covers online-video via her weekly "New Media Minute."

Online-Video Marketing Themes

Tapping Video Community

Online-video creators and viewers are a community that is not shrinking into growing slowly. Your customers are among the online-video viewers, unless you are targeting the approximately 10 to 20 percent of people in the United States who haven't watched an online video.[11] They will watch your advertising and even sometimes spread it for you—unless you promote gratuitously, insult us, or, worse yet, bore us. Some amateurs have built significant audiences, and when they entertain or market, each video is guaranteed to get 10,000 to 200,000 views. That's not a huge number relative to television's reach, but try getting that many views with a video you upload yourself to YouTube.

And here is the best-kept secret. Some online-video stars will promote a brand for a modest fee. While some YouTubers are certifiably nuts, others could be your spokespersons and help you connect with large audiences. Some video creators will make a promotional video for less money than your agency bills you for a lunch meeting; others will do it for free product samples or just kind treatment. Although the scalability of these programs is currently limited (unless you create one of the extremely rare viral sensations), the return on investment is high thanks to cost efficiencies.

Quality of the Video Is Not as Important as You Think

My most popular videos are far from my best, and succeed in a way that is inversely related to the time I put into them. Most of my videos rank in the daily "highest rated" section of the comedy category, yet I am far from the funniest creator on YouTube. Though popular videos tend to be short, funny, and shocking, there are other variables that have as much influence on getting the video seen. Many second- and third-tier sites will give entertaining sponsored videos preferred placement for relatively small amounts of media spend. Got

$10,000? Use the money to help get viewers to watch a clever sponsored video instead of spending it on a fancy, overpriced production (or pouring it into a black hole of unseen banner ads).

THE CAT ON A SKATEBOARD IS MORE INTERESTING THAN YOUR BRAND

While some clever advertisements (with surprise endings, humor, or sex) do become viral, most television ads do not translate well online, and it's a rare promotional video that gets millions of views. Meanwhile, laughing babies and skateboarding cats are all the rage (see Figure 1.7). Rather

Best of Cats Skateboarding

nalts — April 08, 2008 — TVweek's "New Media Minute," hosted by Daisy Whitney, featured a ⊻   **204,861** ⊻
recent interview with YouTube's Jordan Hoffner...   views

Figure 1.7   As marketers we believe our products should be more interesting than cats on skateboard, but audiences beg to differ.

than producing your own viral commercial, it is smarter to sponsor popular video creators. Many creators are making videos with product sponsors or product placement. This does, of course, require marketers to let go of controlling the content; instead, they should trust the instincts of creators to please their audiences.

ONLINE-VIDEO MARKETING DOES NOT REQUIRE A CONTEST

While contests are pervasive tools to engage online-video creators and audiences, they are just one tactic of many. Smarter brands are connecting directly with prominent web-series or online-video stars. These creators have large subscriber bases and fans, and are often delighted to receive sponsorship. I am perplexed why some of the most subscribed YouTube stars don't have sponsors breaking their doors down. I have seen brands pay well into the six figures for videos that get fewer views than some of these creators get each time they post a video.

KEYWORD JUNK TAGGING DOESN'T WORK

Keywords may get your video to rank in searches, but there are far more effective ways to get your videos seen, such as the title of the video, or its thumbnail (the small picture that represents the video). A short funny video with a surprise ending will be exponentially more likely to travel. That said, well-tagged videos may help brands in search. Do a Google search for "Healies" (a misspelling of the shoe called "Heelys") and you may find my "Poor Man Healies" video on the first page of results. (See Figure 1.8.) Meanwhile, Zappos and Dick's Sporting Goods are bidding against the keyword and paying for each click.

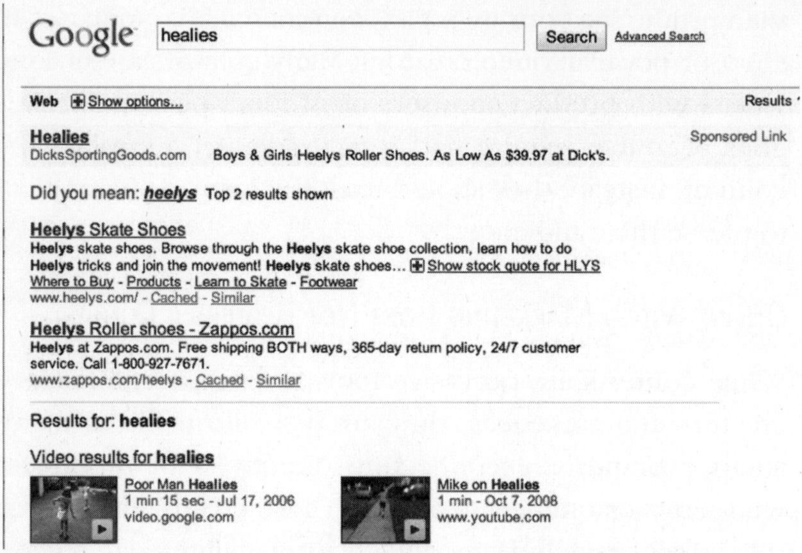

Figure 1.8 Using less competitive terms (like misspellings) in titles and descriptions can work. But bloating tags with popular and unrelated terms is ineffective.

VIRAL DOESN'T MEAN YOU SOLD ANYTHING

Consumers might see your video, but that does not mean they will visit your web site and buy. I learned this the hard way. The conversion rate from viewing a video to visiting a web site, in my experience, is not much better than the low-single digits of direct-response marketing (e-mail or junk mail). That means you either need assumption-based metrics for the positive impact of a view or to hope your video is seen millions of times so the direct-response metrics are not embarrassing.

EXPENSIVE PRODUCTION KILLS ROI

A $250,000 online-video production makes a return on investment difficult. Since fewer than 2 percent of people will visit a web site after a video, a good ROI is dependent on a low production budget and the highest number of views possible.

LOCATION IS AS IMPORTANT AS CONTENT

While at Johnson & Johnson, I would often lament "billboards in the backyard." I used those words to refer to agency-developed micro sites and web sites that had content but no traffic or promotion. The vast majority of online-video viewing, at least for now, occurs on YouTube. Putting your videos on a bloated product.com site is the online equivalent to running television commercials on a kiosk hidden in an abandoned cemetery (or leaving them on that DVD in your file cabinet). (See Figure 1.9.) Your corporate attorneys will express concern because, after all, YouTube is often referred to as the "Wild West." But that's what we said about the Internet in 2000, isn't it?

Figure 1.9   Placing video content on your web site (instead of popular web sites) can be like placing a billboard in your backyard.

CONSERVATIVE ORGANIZATIONS CAN PLAY, TOO

Conservative legal and public-relations policies have prevented many marketers from entering into a dialogue with prominent video creators. Most marketers have seen at least a few videos that mention their own brands or those of competitors, but some brands remain squeamish about something as simple as an online-video contest. Doritos, Dove, Heinz, and Mr. Clean were just a few of the brands that invited consumers to submit to contests to win cash, prizes, fame, or a chance to be on TV. Guess what? They did attract some wacko submissions, but the world didn't end.

Some brands fear running a contest because they don't want to be ridiculed. But disgruntled consumers, via online video, will bash brands whether or not their companies dabble in cyberspace. Quietly watching from the sidelines is no insurance policy against an angry crusade, and passivity certainly won't grow revenue. Ultimately, refraining from using online video out of fear is no smarter than those companies that, more than a decade ago, let their domain names slip away to competitors or angry consumers.

MEASURABILITY IS HERE

As online video continues to mature (the infant still isn't walking yet, but it sure is noisy), it will become almost as measurable as paid searches. For the time being, the most controllable variables are the cost of production and total views. Production costs need to remain low, and the real work starts after the video is uploaded. In addition, the marketing message has to take a backseat to entertainment. I've had sponsors beg for their URL to appear pervasively through a video; however, that tends to alienate viewers and reduce the total views. The rate of viewers who visit the web site is a difficult variable to change unless there's a provocative reason to pry them from their all-you-can-eat video buffet.

LETTING GO: LENNIE SMALL

"I will love my marketing mix, squeeze it, and name it George." Do you recall Lennie Small, the large but limited friend of George Milton in Steinbeck's *Of Mice and Men*? He loved his mouse so much that he squeezed it to death. The more we marketers care about our brand, the easier it is to become Lennie (or the abominable snowman, Hugo, from *Bugs Bunny*). We squeeze some mediums to death, as is evidenced by the omnipresence of branded Facebook pages and online-video contests for condiments. Really, does the world need an online-video contest featuring a brand of mayonnaise?

Marketing, social media, and video entertainment can coexist peacefully. Mass media and push marketing (companies pushing products toward consumers) worked for a while, and it is difficult for us marketers to let it go. When we are passionate about our brand, we like to control the message. Eventually, however, the consumer tunes us out. So, we marketers chase them into the temples of social media using ear-piercing screams of a 30-second pre-roll. We are handing out 25-cent-off coupons at a rave. (I haven't attended a rave yet, but I'm pretty sure nobody's looking for coupons.)

Marketing to Generation ADHD

Many marketers and video creators are accustomed to the relatively higher level of patience of an audience who views film or television. When a viewer is controlling his experience with a mobile device or computer, he rarely tolerates long-form content or advertising. The online-video viewer is leaning forward (versus leaning back while watching television), and is hovering his curser over the "close" or "back" button.

This may change as online video blends with television. But today's online-video viewers have a short attention span, and tend to prefer watching other *people* to watching long-form scripted video or film. I call this "Generation ADHD," and they simply won't sit through pre-rolls unless killer content is behind them. And they won't watch ads unless they're more entertaining and engaging than a stereotypical promotional spot.

We early adopters of online-video watchers are quite unique. A research group queried nearly 2,000 people (representing the U.S. census data) about online-video habits and preferences. The full report, created by Frank N. Magid Associates and sponsored by Metacafe, is called "Opportunities in Online Video."[12] The basic information is consistent with other research in the field, but here are four important factors:

1. Nearly half of us (45 percent) said online-video ads are as acceptable as television ads.

2. Males, age 18 to 34, preferred online video and the Web nearly two to three times more often than television (keep that in mind if you're punishing your teenager).

3. Thirty percent of 55- to 65-year-olds watch online video weekly, which dispels a lot of skepticism of marketers that this audience is not consuming online

video. While 70 percent of males ages 18 to 24 watch online video weekly, the peak range for females was 12 to 17 (56 percent watch weekly).

4. Those of us who view video online at least weekly (approximately 43 percent) are significantly different from non-online-video watchers (around 30 percent). We're twice as a likely to own an iPhone, purchase virtual goods, and carry a music player. And we're significantly more likely to be an online gamer and rent DVDs.

5. Just as it occurred with the Internet, the audience for online video will continue to resemble the general population. In the coming years, however, marketers should consider not whether their audience is watching online video, but what vehicles are most efficient and scalable to reach them.

Until online video is more easily consumed via mobile devices and television, it is important to adapt video content to this ADHD generation. Compel them early, focus on entertainment and not just on promotion, and ensure that the marketing message isn't at the end of the video.

So You Still Want to Go Viral?

As I have mentioned, marketers and advertisers have a range of more productive applications for online video than the clichéd and increasingly difficult viral video. While early "stealth marketing" campaigns were able to increase brand awareness through viral videos, the increasing proliferation of online videos means that few individual ones are penetrating our collective consciousness as "Numa Numa" did in 2006.

Still, one of the most predictable questions I face when speaking or appearing in media is, "What makes video go viral?"

The honest answer is one that satisfies few: It's largely unpredictable, and I view with skepticism anyone who promises to know the "secret sauce." There are, of course, common attributes among videos that have been

Lady Gaga - Bad Romance
189,429,591 views
LadyGagaVEVO

Charlie bit my finger - again !
182,655,664 views
HDCYT

Evolution of Dance
142,035,737 views
judsonlaipply

Pitbull - I Know You Want Me (Ca...
116,811,375 views
UltraRecords

Miley Cyrus - 7 Things - Officia...
116,578,832 views
hollywoodrecords

Hahaha
116,360,788 views
BlackOleg

Lady Gaga - Just Dance ft. Colby...
107,824,012 views
LadyGagaVEVO

Lo que tú Quieras Oír
100,514,580 views
kaejane

Justin Bieber - Baby ft. Ludacris
98,648,572 views
JustinBieberVEVO

Figure 1.10 While commercial videos have gone "viral," the most-viewed videos have a few common traits: music, dancing, attractive women, pranks, and children.

popularized, and I outline them in Chapter 3. The common traits (see Figure 1.10 for some of the most-viewed YouTube videos in history) are: music, dancing, attractive women, candid-camera-style pranks, children, and topical and political references.

CHAPTER 2

Flavors of Video

From Skateboarding Cats to Pro

In this chapter, you will learn:

- That there is a large continuum between *professional* video and *user-generated* content.

- That a *third hidden layer* offers marketers a cost-efficient and powerful opportunity to get messages woven into the video.

- How marketers can cost-efficiently market via popular content, going beyond banner ads without complex partnerships with major studios and networks.

There is a quality continuum of online videos, yet this is often misunderstood because we instinctively polarize them into professional (network) content and user-generated content (UGC). There are, in fact, many flavors of content in between.

As viewers, advertisers, and even video creators, we have bifurcated video into two extremes. From Oprah to "sneezing panda bear." From *Lost* to "the giggling infant." And from *The Office* to "monkey smelling its finger."

31

The Three Flavors of Online-Video Content

Flavor 1: Professional Content (vanilla and chocolate: the only "safe" place to advertise). Advertisers, when they're not convincing marketers to create their own content, are often urging them to buy advertisements around so-called safe, professional content. We don't see as many ads swarming around such classic user-generated content (UGC) as cats riding skateboards, or dogs using toilets. We are seeing an influx of ad dollars into the online-video medium, and it is trending upward while most of the marketing mix is declining. Given the rapid increase of dollars being allocated to professional content, only two things can happen: The professional content will have to increase its audiences dramatically or advertising prices will rise, or both.

Flavor 2: User-Generated Content (nutty coconut: the cheap buy). UGC offers much lower advertising costs, so you can reach a wider audience efficiently. You can target specific niches or demographics, and the UGC viewers are, frankly, easier to distract from their content. Want to get someone to respond to your stupid "shoot the monkey" banner ad? You'll have better luck on a web site for weather or gaming. More professional content, as in the *Wall Street Journal*, tends to attract more affluent viewers, but they are less easy to hijack with our silly ads. That being said, I always want to know where my ads will land. When I was at Johnson & Johnson, I didn't want to get a call from the CEO because my banner landed inadvertently on Crazymeds.org due to Google's network of content.

Flavor 3: The Hidden Online-Video Flavor (rainbow surprise: efficient and targeted). The hidden flavor is the overlooked one between professional content and UGC, so

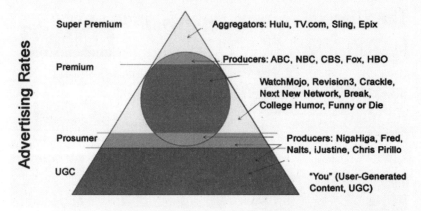

Image by Ashkan Karbasfrooshan, 2010 (modified for legibility)

Figure 2.1   Advertising revenue and video quality tiers.

I've decided to call it the hidden layer because it's so often overlooked.

Consider another way of displaying these flavors based on the monetary value. Figure 2.1 shows financial implications (ad rates and profitability index) of various flavors. The image, created by Ashkan Karbasfrooshan, suggests that profitability will belong not to leading aggregators of super premium content, nor user-generated content. Rather the premium producers (emerging digital studios, aggregators, and solo producers) command decent advertising rates but also keep costs in line with the medium. Karbasfrooshan has written extensively about this evolving ecosystem and is the CEO of WatchMojo, a producer, publisher, and syndicator of video content for broadband platforms.

Examples of the Hidden Third Layer

Consider three examples of this delicious third flavor.

1. Digital Studios. Some are calling them the "New Establishment," but I prefer to consider them digital studios,

Figure 2.2   Sometimes called the "New Establishment," a number of studios have formed to create or aggregate video primarily for the Web.

because they are generally producers, aggregators, and distributors of video content for broadband. These create, aggregate, or commission semi-pro short-form video content, and promote it across various online-video sites and increasingly through new devices (like TiVo, Apple TV, and software installed on Web-enabled televisions). Many of these companies have gone bust, and we will continue to see new ones appear, existing ones die, and ultimately, a consolidation. Currently, they include (see Figure 2.2) Next New Networks, 15 Gigs, Mondo, Funny or Die, Take180, Machinima, Revision3, Demand Media, Watch Mojo, For Your Imagination, and My Damned Channel. These studios are often tailoring video content to the early adopters of online video (technical enthusiasts, video gamers, animators, film creators, social-media participants).

To date, fewer have succeeded in creating and popularizing web series that would appeal to general audiences. There are exceptions: Neil Patrick Harris's "Dr. Horrible's Sing-Along Blog" by Mutant Enemy Productions evolved from a web series to a DVD sold at many retailers. Felicia Day, who appeared in Dr. Horrible, escalated her own career by writing, producing, and acting in "The Guild," a series about online gamers that is distributed by Xbox Live and Microsoft and sponsored by Sprint. Next New Networks' "Barely Political" (featuring the ubiquitous "Obama Girl") is approaching a half billion views.

2. Individual Stars. If a popular YouTube Partner has a significant following of video game enthusiasts, we might agree that it's an incredibly smart place to promote the Wii or acne cream. There is an abundance of advertising inventory in that hidden flavor. Fred (Lucas Cruikshank)—one of the most popular kids on YouTube—draws more daily views than many prime-time television shows. More important, the aggregated views of even a few top amateur online-video stars far surpass those of prime-time television shows (see Figure 2.3). For example, Dane Boedigheimer, creator of Annoying Orange and Gagfilms, was viewed

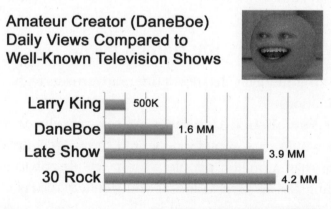

Source: Nielsen & Tubemogul.com, April 2010

Figure 2.3 Some individual amateur "webstars" command daily audiences that rival well-known television shows. DaneBoe (Dane Boedigheimer) is creator of Gagfilms and Annoying Orange.[1]

50 million times in April 2010 (approximately 1.6 million times daily). Increasingly, YouTube is providing advertisers with tools to isolate those audiences, may it be via specific marketing techniques, appealing to the greater good with activist videos, or simple adolescent pranks. It is difficult, but important, to focus not on the content, but the audience. While top brands have valid "taste and tone" guidelines, far too many brands obsess with the video content itself rather than the audience.

3. Hyper-Niche Content. If Yahoo! Video created a round-the-clock "Lindsay Lohan Online-Video Show," that's where you'd want to sell your latest Lindsay Lohan action figure (handcuff accessories sold separately). This hypothetical channel, while not necessarily worthy of professional production, would certainly qualify as being more targeted than UGC. The video content would not necessarily need to be professionally produced, and arguably, you would want to keep costs down to $200 per minute until you confirm that an audience exists.

Advertising via the Hidden Flavor

Now, this hidden video flavor offers advertisers eight unique distinctions.

1. Established Audiences. No smart producer or advertiser would try to build a new Fred show. Fred already has more than a million people who have subscribed and are waiting for his next video. If you pitched YouTube's Fred to NBC two years ago, you would have been tossed from the building. Would you rather roll the dice by shooting a viral video, developing branded entertainment, or simply leverage Fred to reach an existing audience. It's an unfair analogy, but my own videos attract daily views that exceed the monthly views of most product.com web sites I've marketed (even with $100,000 monthly paid-search campaigns).

2. Audience Influence. Viewers consume their online-video shows and stars like zombies in pursuit of a brain. It is an indisputable fact. If Fred started wearing Madonna rings on his wrist, they would be back in style. The cultlike following of some of the popular video channels and people has influence that is greater than is suggested by the reach, if measured in television terms.

3. Quality. It's not professional and TV-like, but it's good enough for the audience. Many people develop "parasocial" friendships with online video creators, where they have a sense of intimacy with the webstar even though they haven't met. Many viewers would rather watch their "parasocial friend" rant about the news via his webcam than watch another boring sitcom or reality show in high definition. If you trust audiences will eventually migrate to quality content, please reexamine what *quality* means in this medium.

4. Relevance. Ad targeting is easier as we move deeper into amateur content. "The Onion" has brilliant common-denominator comedy, but "You Suck at Photoshop" (a mock video instruction series depicted in Figure 2.4) probably has a more specified demographic that can help a brand target. Do you want to reach people who celebrate their adolescence (at any age) or soccer moms? Relevance is easier now that video content and audiences are growing and fragmenting. If you want to use the Internet to sell toe-fungus medicine, there are specific sites on which you could advertise. You would likely advertise on a toe-fungus blog before you launch a "run of site" media campaign on a health and wellness web site. There are reasons why Google

You Suck at Photoshop #4: Paths and Masks

This is a video response to You Suck at Photoshop #5: Select Color Range

★★★★⯪ 7,102 ratings   1,377,229 views

Figure 2.4   As an example of a show targeting a specific audience, My Damned Channel's "You Suck at Photoshop" is a comedic series that teaches photo-editing software.

text advertisements outperform almost any targeted display media buy. They are relevant, targeted, and timely. Unfortunately, this makes an ad buyer's job quite complex and will require more creative treatments than television. But advertisers take note: This means we marketers will need more than three versions of our 60-second spot (you know—the white guy, the gay guy, and the Hispanic/African American). And if creative budgets don't get bigger, amateur video creators are well poised to be the fallbacks.

5. Ad-Safe Content. Unlike regular UGC, most of the hidden video flavor content is filtered to be ad friendly (YouTube Partners, for example, get dumped if they break terms of service rules, like being foul or violating copyright laws). Those rules are as true for little ole me as they are for the Universal Music Group's popular channel on YouTube.

6. Economic Sustainability. Most amateur stars have low costs. Many individuals are making a comfortable living, while higher-cost studios are struggling. As advertisers, we would rather make deals with individuals or studios that are profitable, rather than those that are cost-prohibitive for the medium.

7. Cost-Efficient Spends. We can saturate Fred's YouTube channel with video advertisements, or work with him and YouTube on a customized program that does far more than ads alone. Premium video creators, by contrast, are destined to charge higher CPMs given their higher cost structure. Likewise, it's not as easy for these providers to create custom content for an advertiser.

8. Scale. The deeper advertisers go into the long tail of video content, the better their chances of being able to broaden and scale campaigns without sacrificing targeting and relevance. We may temporarily saturate some niches, but if there is an audience and advertiser demand, then new creators will emerge to fill the void.

There is gold in those niche hills.

Pros versus Amateurs

Currently, YouTube does not overtly distinguish between professionals and amateurs in its Partner program, or in the way it alleges to promote videos. But I expect this to change, and it's an important sign that YouTube may be transforming from a user-generated platform to a professional media distributor.

Today, advertisers have two choices: They can buy inexpensive and underperforming banners that run across user-generated content (cat videos), or select "advertiser safe" aside Partner content through such programs as

home-page takeovers or targeted display ads. YouTube Partners include professional creators (CBS, NBA, National
Geographic, Discovery, and Jonas Brothers) as well as amateur webstars, whom we'll discuss later.

For advertisers—and audiences—there is no material
difference between the videos made by the BBC and a
guy like one of the 10 most-subscribed Partners, most of
whom are amateurs. The only stratification that occurs on
YouTube is between those that qualify as Partners and those
that don't (we'll call that user-generated content). Some
choosy ad buyers may currently handpick channels, but
that's a manual and painstaking undertaking. More likely,
media buyers care less about the content itself and more
about targeting their demographics—regardless of whether
the 18- to 25-year-old male is watching the Jonas Brothers
or Fred.

The original and core audience of YouTube arrived
to escape professional content, and they embrace
amateurs.

As we know, the vast majority of views on YouTube are
of content that cannot be well monetized into profitable
margins (user-generated, non-Partner content). Really only
a small fraction of total views (but most of its revenue)
comes from ads surrounding the Partners. Among those
Partners, the current most popular three YouTube channels belong to true amateurs: Fred, Nigahiga, and Smosh. As
the "most subscribed" list progresses, we've seen the rise
of some professional content like Universal Music and the
Jonas Brothers, but they're still the minority among the top
100. But again, the current advertising model largely treats
these amateurs and professionals similarly. . . . The standards
are the same (copyright and taste/tone), and the cost is the
same (per impression).

If YouTube segments professional content from the mass community of YouTube stars, that's a nontrivial move. On one hand, I like that I might rise on the "most subscribed" list to a presumably higher spot among community videos (which will presumably exclude professionals). On the other hand, it could mean that new viewers to YouTube are steered to professional content, which could have some negative implications for amateurs. I have often speculated on the costs and benefits of segmenting pro versus amateur content, and it has significant implications for amateurs.

Some insight garnered from a discussion I had with a media-purchasing colleague at my previous employer (Merck & Company) may help you appreciate the confusion. She was aware of my YouTube hobby, and told me some of Merck's brands would be buying ads on professional content. Then she smiled and said it wouldn't be placed on the content I create (which she assumed fell into the user-generated layer). I had to inform her that I was, in fact, a YouTube Partner, and urged her to avoid placing ads on my video due to potential conflict of interest. Partners are Partners, even if it's possible that premium Partners command slightly higher advertising rates because they are perceived as safer.

If YouTube segments the content for viewers, will it soon craft different ad deals for professionals versus amateurs? Could that change the ad rate and tempt buyers to restrain their ad spending to professional movies, shows, and music? If so, YouTube can charge a higher premium, but will have far less content and inventory in these sections—at least initially.

The bulk of YouTube's core audience will find this segmentation offensive, evidence that YouTube has abandoned community and is turning into a bigger Hulu.com. But one can't fault YouTube for wanting to attract a higher level of content to appeal to broader audiences. And that content may command advertising dollars that might otherwise flow to AOL, Yahoo!, MSN, or even Hulu.

Ultimately, the segmentation, however, is less interesting than the answers to the following five questions. Rest assured we cannot expect YouTube to answer these soon.

1. What will delineate *shows* from *community*? Can an amateur have a show, or is that just for pro content?

2. Will the pro content provide channel owners special features, more interesting functionality, and better monetization options? We're already seeing special functionality for folks like Oprah.

3. Will the precious YouTube home page promote the pros over the amateurs, because the former might attract premium advertisers and may attract a more mainstream audience?

4. How will YouTube continue to differentiate itself from alternative channels for professional content, and will studios distribute clips or full episodes (hoping to still migrate audiences to properties where they retain greater control of revenue)?

5. Most important, will this transformation change dynamics between YouTube (still the largest video distributor by a distance) and professional creators, networks, and distributors?

CHAPTER 3
Viral Video Is Dead

In this chapter, you will learn:

- Why advertisers creating viral videos are likely wasting money and missing more proven tactics.

- The "Seven Deadly Sins" marketers often make in naive attempts to make their brand viral.

- The eight immutable laws of viral video.

- The common traits of the most popular online videos (from kids and pets to dancing and topical satire).

Why Viral Video Is Dead

For reasons I cannot quite explain, I am often invited to speak in Canada. After an all-night drive to Toronto, I leapt onstage last year at the Canadian Marketing Association annual meeting. I proclaimed that viral video was dead, and the country's marketing magazine led with an article titled "Marketing Week Begins with 'Viral Is Dead' Declaration."

It is true that in 2005 through 2007, many clever advertisements went viral, and were passed along in the millions. While this is increasingly rare, advertisers still recommend viral video to their clients. As I mentioned in an earlier chapter, it is, in fact, a misnomer to refer to a video as *viral* until it actually *goes viral*.

Creating a video in hopes for it to go viral is the gambler's equivalent of roulette. The payoff may be significant, but the odds are very low. There will continue to be exceptions like the Evian Roller Babies (an ad featuring digitally animated babies roller skating to rock music).

Certain professional creators, and even more amateur video creators, have large, recurring audiences and fans. So their sponsored videos are far more likely to travel the Web and be seen by millions. Two of my Fox Broadcasting videos, created through a campaign that included a dozen stars, surpassed 1 million views each (for *Fringe* and *Lie to Me*). The target of the entire campaign was 8 million views; Figure 3.1 shows some examples of the videos.

I encourage marketers to choose the more efficient and guaranteed approaches—through advertising, public

Figure 3.1 More than 8 million people watched online videos promoting Fox Broadcasting's *Fringe* and *Lie to Me*. The campaign, conducted by Hitviews, involved dozens of webstars.

relations, or partnering with a person or content network that already has an audience. Certain online-video studios and amateur video creators have large, recurring audiences and fans. Their sponsored videos are far more likely to travel the Web and be seen by millions.

Seven Deadly Sins of Viral Video

Show me a marketer without viral on his marketing plan and I'll show you an online-video site that is profitable. Push marketing, the act of insisting a viewer watches an advertisement, is losing its impact. Time-shifted television viewing (via TiVo and digital-video recorders) has given individuals the ability to skip commercials. Top television shows are losing viewers to other mediums, and audiences are fragmenting. Even online advertising is getting more difficult, with paid-search prices rising and banner clickthroughs dropping. Given the low variable cost of viral, it's natural that advertisers want to give it a shot.

It is far more difficult than it appears to compel a wide audience to promote your product by sharing an online video. However, if you insist upon trying, save yourself some money and time by avoiding the "Seven Deadly Sins of Advertising via Viral Video."

1. Make a white and brown cow. Author Seth Godin has a term called *Purple Cow*, which refers to marketing that is "remarkable," and compels people to pay attention and share it with others. Your online video needs to be Technicolor Purple if you actually expect it to break through an increasingly crowded space. Naturally, the odds increase if the video is shocking, controversial, sexy, quirky, or funny. However, that sometimes defies the character of a product or service. Is the short-term viral payoff worth the potential of undermining a brand's positioning?

2. Pretend you're not advertising. Nothing quite irritates a consumer like being secretly persuaded. "Al Gore's Penguin Army" is a classic example of a funny video that was exposed as having a public-relations agenda. Transparency is important in online video and social media.

3. Spend a fortune on production. It pains me to see companies dump huge production budgets into online video. I have seen it pay off only a few times. One example was Smirnoff's "Tea Partay" (see Figure 3.2), which did go viral and get media pickup, but clearly was not a low-budget production. It perplexes me to see marketers engage professionals to create authentic and rough-around-the-edges video. There are already video creators who can achieve the same look at a budget that is less than the cost of a lunch

Figure 3.2 Tea Partay, a rap song promoting Smirnoff's malt beverages, is an increasingly rare example of a professionally produced viral video.

meeting with an agency and producer. Improvisational acting, sloppy camera moves, and poor production can actually give a video that feel of consumer-generated video. There is a growing market for individual directors who can shoot online videos for around $10 to $50,000. When Yahoo! featured on its home page my "Lay Me Off" video (which I've temporarily pulled down at the request of some of my fellow employees), I got a number of e-mails from people asking how much I'd charge for a viral video for their clients. A marketer is more likely to reach a positive return on investment (ROI) by avoiding a fixed-cost investment in production.

4. Tell consumers instead of engaging them. It is important to avoid thinking about an online video as an adaptation of a 60-second advertisement. Obviously the video has got to be irreverent, weird, funny, and different. More important, the Web has the ability to make the viral video a dialogue. Contests are one approach, but there are other ways to engage an audience into more content, interactive polls, and community.

5. Sponsor a video contest because everyone else is doing it. The online-video contest fad will continue, but it will become more difficult to activate consumers to promote your product. If you search "video contest" on Google, you may find dozens of advertisements for contests. To give you an idea of how abused such contests are getting, there was, one summer, a promotion by a *mayonnaise* manufacturer looking for videos about recipes. A marketer invests in online video to promote a product or service, and video contests can sometimes achieve that goal. However, contests are often video tactics in search of a strategy.

6. Expect them to buy after they see your video. Many marketers have great expectations about the behavior that will ensue after someone watches their viral video.

I have seen many agencies estimate that 10 to 20 percent will visit a web site or purchase a product. In fact, only a very small portion of people (between 2 and 10 percent in the many campaigns I have analyzed) will take immediate action. In the years ahead, we'll be able to measure action that isn't immediate, but in the near term, a dose of realism is wise. Certain technologies allow web sites to access an Internet browser's history file and identify what sites an individual visited before making a purchase. Some early studies show that a percentage of viewers of, for instance, a Nike viral video, returned later to a search engine and typed Nike to make a purchase.

7. Throw in the towel. Many marketers try viral, fail, and then decide online video doesn't work. As a result, they retrench to traditional online advertising. I urge marketers not to abandon the medium because a viral tactic failed. The online-video sites are mostly new, and there is an unlimited possibility for creative partnerships that exceeds the impact of banners and pre-rolls. Even YouTube, which was slower to embrace commercial interests, has constant new offerings for advertisers. These include sophisticated targeting tools, branded entertainment, and sponsored channels.

The Eight Immutable Laws of Viral Video

I've always loved the certainty of the title *The 22 Immutable Laws of Marketing*, so I'm borrowing the phrase from authors Al Ries and Jack Trout.

1. The definition of viral video is that it goes viral. No online video can be called *viral* until it actually goes viral. A video can be defined as going viral if it is shared significantly, and that bar keeps rising. If a video is seen 5 to 10 million times in a one-week period, and receives

Figure 3.3 Author's most-viewed video, "Scary Maze," took minutes to create, but prank with engaging thumbnail drove it to nearly 20 million views.

significant media and social-media coverage, it's fair to call it viral.

2. A viral video does not have to be good. They are often humorous and sometimes "ripped" from television (Like *Saturday Night Live's* "Lazy Sunday" rap parody[1]). Celebrity scandals, eyewitness accounts, and whistleblowing also make good viral candidates.

3. Nobody can predict what becomes viral. My videos that have achieved modest viral status (like my inane "Scary Maze" pictured in Figure 3.3, which has exceeded 15 million views[2]) are almost never the ones I expect. I am often asked what makes a video viral, and I can point to some commonalities (short, funny, engaging, captivating introduction, surprise twist, sexy, unexpected, temper tantrums, mistakes or "fails," candid moments, shock).

4. If you are trying to advertise via viral, dial down the marketing. One example of a relatively successful corporate campaign was Office Max's "Elf Yourself"[3] (which allowed you to place your photo over dancing elves). This had utility and was fun for people to share. A less successful campaign, with just a few million views driven mostly from paid advertisements, was "Penny Pranks,"[4] in which

LEAVE BRITNEY ALONE!

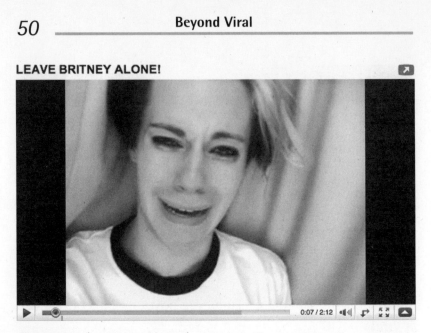

0:07 / 2:12

Figure 3.4   Chris Crocker developed overnight fame with his tear-filled defense of Britney Spears.

a guy tried to buy things with pennies. I pulled this prank at a tollbooth[5] two years earlier, so I was glad to see the campaign fail.

5. Topical is important. Viral is subject to "pile on," whereby one viral explosion creates copycats. A clip is more likely to be discovered if it contains keywords from other viral videos that are being searched. When YouTuber Chris Crocker (see Figure 3.4) cried and screamed "Leave Britney Alone!" in reaction to media coverage of Britney Spears, the video was poorly rated but seen in excess of 30 million times. Countless parodies ensued, but the joke became old quickly.

6. New viral ideas rarely derive from old ones. Most viral videos are unique, and so imitating one typically doesn't work. However, to track viral videos, you can explore Unruly Media's "Viral Video Chart"[6] or consult *Ad Age's* "Viral Video Chart,"[7] which tracks commercial videos that range from a few hundred thousand views to a million.

7. Duration of video is vital. Short videos will always outperform long ones. Some studies have shown that as many as 90 percent of viewers will watch for less than 10 seconds.[8] Stay under a minute for best results, and avoid going beyond three minutes. I saw a recent Coke "Happy Vending Machine" campaign that dragged the viewer through 30 painful seconds before anything interesting happened. I'm guessing I'm in the 35 percent that survived to the payoff.

8. Cheaters never win (at least in the long run). If a company promises you it can "make" your video viral, it's probably manipulating views. TechCrunch ran an article by Dan Ackerman Greenberg,[9] arguing that viral videos are a result of someone who "worked hard to make it happen—some company like mine." He then detailed some of the tricks that he uses to run "clandestine marketing campaigns meant to ensure that promotional videos became truly viral." Weeks later I wrote a piece for AdAge.com titled "Ten Lessons for Marketers Using Viral Videos."[10] I was tickled to find a blogger (SocialTNT) refer to Ackerman as the Wicked Witch of the West and to me as Glinda the Good Witch.[11]

What Makes Videos Go Viral?

I hope by now we can all agree that your brand alone will not create a viral sensation. It is important for marketers, advertisers, and creators to know what sticks. I am horrible about e-mail, but was elated when Ben Relles, creator of "Obama Girl" (see Figure 3.5) sent me a note years ago. He was everywhere, and I was flattered that he wanted to compare notes. Surprisingly, he was interested in learning

Figure 3.5 "Obama Girl" by BarelyPolitical.com, is a viral sensation driven by a proven formula in June 2007: attractive woman, song parody, and topicality.

how I had grown my YouTube channel. Ben left a career in advertising and marketing because he didn't see his clients deploying the recipe he knew would work. So, he combined the most popular traits of videos at that time—topicality, politics, song, and attractive women—into video content that had no small role in Obama's overnight visibility. I am not suggesting that had "Obama Girl" not rocked the nation in 2007 and 2008 we would have a different president. But I like to refer to Ben's wife as "the woman behind the man behind the woman behind the president."

Ben and I have two things in common. We are both career marketers, and we obsessively track the trends in the most-popular videos. The following list describes the commonalities of the most-viewed YouTube videos. It is based on what I learned from Ben, and from a simple review of YouTube's most popular videos (by day, month, or history).

Pranks. My two most-popular videos are pranks: "Farting in Public"[12] shows my nephew's friend, Spencer, using a fart machine to elicit stares in a library. It was featured on YouTube's home page when it mattered, in March 2007 (see Figure 3.6). But my farting opus has since been eclipsed by "Scary Maze Game"[13] a 52-second prank I almost chose not to post but continues to get millions and millions of views. My wife's friend (who, incidentally, introduced the two of us with the promise of us being future husband and wife) brought her three sons to visit. I put her son on a web-site game that requires careful navigation of the mouse through mazes. Before you complete the maze, the screen erupts with a scream and a photo of an image, presumably from *The Exorcist*.

Another wildly popular video, "Scary Hitchhiker Prank," which I have since removed from YouTube out of guilt, featured YouTube prankster EdBassmaster pretending to be a convict to whom I offer a car ride. Spencer, who thought he would be making a drive-through prank, was, indeed, terrified as EdBassmaster described how he recently "shanked" someone in prison. Indeed, the YouTube audiences enjoy the realism and shock of a good prank. Some of my pranks (like a huge frog I used to scare my wife on a Bermuda vacation) have appeared on MTV's *Pranked*, which does not take unsolicited pranks but features some of the best. (See Figure 3.6.)

Dancing. It's no coincidence that one of the most-viewed YouTube videos of all time features a diverse and entertaining dancing routine. "Evolution of Dance," by Judson Laipply, is engaging and nostalgic.

Music. *Britain's Got Talent* singer Susan Boyle was propelled to international visibility in April 2009, partially because a video of her song performance was widely

Huge Frog Scares Wife (as seen on MTV Pranked)

Nalts 🔊 861 videos ⌄ Subscribe

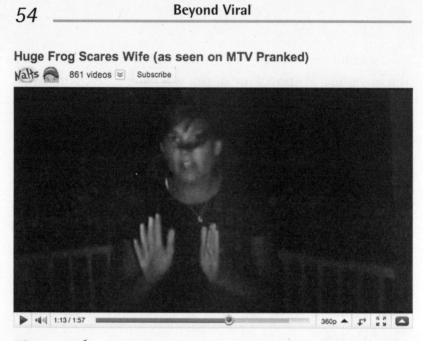

▶ ◀) 1:13 / 1:57 ━━━━━━━━━━━━━━━━━━━━━━⦿━━━━━━━━ 360p ▲ ↳ ⤢ ◳

Figure 3.6 A huge frog gave "Nalts" an opportunity to terrify his wife on a vacation in Bermuda. The clip was later licensed by MTV's *Pranked* and aired nationally.

circulated on YouTube. See her most popular video and you'll appreciate why an unknown Scottish singer captivated so many individuals. Most of the online-video "most-viewed videos of all time" highlight professional or amateur singers.

Children. "Charlie Bit My Finger," which shows a young British child biting the finger of his brother (see Figure 3.7), is one of the most-viewed videos of all time, and the subject of countless parodies and homages. Who can resist the video titled "HaHaHa," featuring the unbridled and contagious giggles of a child amused by an adult's funny sounds. Or the "serious face" of a child mimicking his mother? Videos that include children seem to resonate with viewers. I believe that my four children are no small part of why I have been viewed so many times. And Shay Butler may be funny alone, but his "tard" children provide some wonderful moments.

Charlie bit my finger - again !

★★★★☆ 409,663 ratings

165,944,070 views

Figure 3.7 "Charlie Bit My Finger" is one of YouTube's most-viewed videos, and shows a British child patiently being bitten by his toddler brother.

Political Humor. Even those who dismiss the success of "Obama Girl" to luck acknowledge that it has become a franchise. Ben Relles has kept his Barely Political channel vibrant far beyond Obama's election using a magical mix of topicality, pretty women, and musical satire. His "I've Got a Crush on Obama" has won numerous awards for its viral appeal. Mr. Relles is the only other successful YouTube creator who shares my background in marketing and advertising. When Sarah Palin emerged as a vice-presidential candidate in the summer of 2008, I dressed in drag for a parody of *Tootsie*.[14] The video (see Figure 3.8) was seen less than a million times, but appeared on CNN and other news sites.

Fails. What is it about a pratfall, blooper, or embarrassing mistake that is so intriguing? The term *fail* has become a universal phrase for "the opposite of success,"

Figure 3.8   Well-timed political satire gave the author and his fellow YouTube creators national coverage on CNN. A report included "Nalts" and Tina Fey doing Sarah Palin impersonations during the 2008 election.

and has resulted in its own Wikipedia page. One of my favorite YouTube channels is "Failblog," which offers an endless stream of short, hysterical goofs. The channel is not monetized by the creators (see Failblog's blog), since the clips are usually ripped without permission from television or other sources. So while it's not highly profitable, it is hard not to binge on these videos like popcorn. If your video's title simply includes the word *fail*, it might get more views.

Music and Song Parody. The number one most-subscribed YouTube female musician of all time, "Venetian Princess,"[15] has made a career of song parodies. Her song parodies of the likes of Lady Gaga, Miley Cyrus, and Katy Perry have been seen tens of millions of times, and her most popular video is a satire of Britney Spears's "Womanizer."

Vlogging. For every vlogger (video blogger) who has achieved most-subscribed status, there are millions of others hiding in the depths of the YouTube ocean. But the active viewers of YouTube want to connect personally with a video creator, and poorly edited moments of life intrigue them. Don't ask me to explain it. I would never have imagined in 2005 that this would be true today. But some of my YouTube friends simply pull out their "Flip" cameras (a small, simple and low-cost video camera) and show life moments, and their fans would go to battle for them. Sometimes I forget that there is a crowd, perhaps larger than would fit in the New Orleans Superdome, which has followed my life for the past years. When I asked them in a recent video to help remind me to write this book, I faced weeks of comments on my video that said "WRITE YOUR BOOK." Thanks, viewers!

How To. While "do it yourself" (DYI) is not the most popular content, it is well poised for profit. Howcast (see

Figure 3.9 Howcast, founded by a Google Video alumnus, uses freelancers and small budgets to satisfy high demand for instructional videos.

Figure 3.9) is a site that is devoted exclusively to short, to-the-point "how to" content that is well optimized on search engines, and is mostly "evergreen" (as opposed to topical) humor. The number of search-engine queries that add the terms *how to* have been on a steady rise.

CHAPTER 4

Video's Role in the Marketing Funnel

In this chapter, you will learn:

- How video can serve as the stage of a customer-engagement process, from awareness through trial and loyalty.

- The best practices for engaging with prospects after they've seen your video.

- Three primary types of online video: viral (awareness), conversion (initiation), and education (loyalty).

- How video can help humanize a corporation, and mitigate media's tendency to vilify or characterize its public image.

For every marketer there seems to exist a different definition of the *marketing funnel*, which is meant to describe the path from a target customer's awareness to loyalty. Most consider online video's role at the top of this funnel (awareness or engagement), but miss opportunities to use online video to complement relationships with prospects and customers.

Although it is increasingly easy for a business to create a destination web site with social-media tools and embedded videos, it's important to populate content where people already travel. Again, these "billboards in their backyard" won't drive sales.

Still, having videos on your site can help visitors turn to prospects and even customers, and that's something harder to control on a third-party web site like YouTube. This book emphasizes video at the top of the funnel because that is where businesses need the most help. However, a web site that doesn't convert attention to purchase is like fishing with a net full of holes.

From Curiosity to Close: A Customer Case Study

Imagine the following real example of a customer searching Google, and being compelled via video to make a $10,000 purchase.

- Paul wants a home office, but there is no room in his house and he needs a work area that is quiet and separate. He searches Google for terms like *prefab home*, *mobile office*, *shed*, and *pool house*.

- He finds a do-it-yourself video on YouTube by a guy who is building his own office loft. Since Paul wants a freestanding structure, he looks away and notices a YouTube video thumbnail under "promoted videos" that shows a factory-assembled pool house. He clicks the ad, costing the advertiser maybe 5 to 10 cents.

- The ad launches a promotional video on YouTube, which showcases the various structures made by Amish carpenters nearby. Paul realizes that it may be a faster and only slightly more expensive way to solve his problem. The company's web site is listed in the video's description, and he clicks the URL in the description (costing the advertiser nothing).

- The company, unfortunately, seems to specialize in horse barns, storage sheds, and chicken coops. He's turned off by that, and finds nothing about offices in the menu or primary navigation. But before he returns to Google, he happens to see a photo of "sheds/pool houses."

- On the pool house page (see Figure 4.1), he clicks on a video titled "instant home office," and it shows how the manufacturer can adapt a pool house into a ready-made office for around $8,000. It completes the project with wiring, an electrical box, and drywall.

- Paul likes the idea, knowing he'll probably spend weeks building it himself and spend at least $4,000 on lumber and equipment. He calls the company, and by the end of the phone call has upgraded to a $10,000 home office.

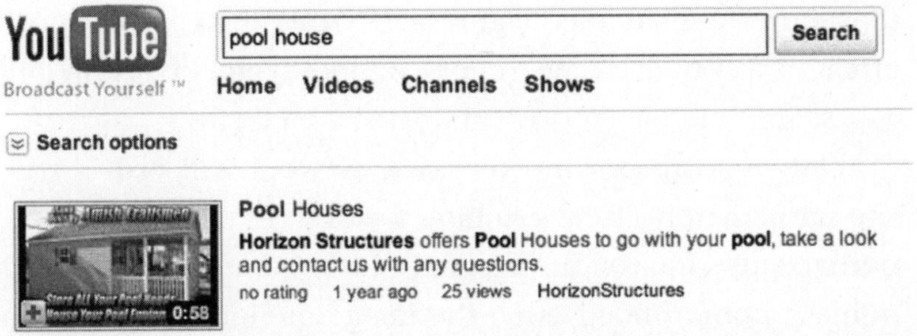

Figure 4.1 Horizon structures uses videos to reach prospective buyers via YouTube, the second most popular search engine after Google.

- The company, of course, asks him how he learned about them. His response, "your web site," tells the marketer precious little about the experience.

Video served two vital roles in capturing this individual's attention and closing the deal (or at least convincing the prospect to call). First, the video advertisement was well targeted to the do-it-yourself individual who is price sensitive but might easily be persuaded to save some time. The ad took him to another YouTube video, which compelled him to visit the manufacturer's web site for an ad spend of nickels rather than dollars via paid search.

The manufacturer also used video to save him from abandoning a purchase because the web site was focused on farmers. Despite the company's mostly irrelevant product line, Paul eventually found a video that addressed his specific needs.

Driving Traffic via YouTube

Marketers often fail to realize the criticality to posting their videos on YouTube even if they're on a product web site. This can increase the views of the videos and drive traffic to the product site (see Figure 4.2). YouTube can be a cost-efficient way to drive awareness, but not typically as efficient as a search engine to drive traffic to a web site.

Only a small portion of video viewers will visit a web site immediately after watching a video (in my experience, perhaps just one to four percent). I try to communicate this point at conferences using the image in Figure 4.3. If your marketing goal, however, is dependent on getting someone to your web site, then there are some ways to increase the odds. Most people think that YouTube video creators

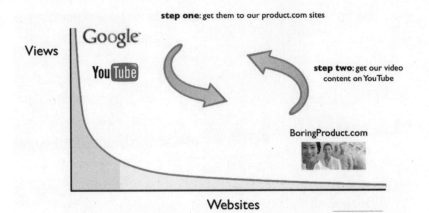

Figure 4.2 The majority of Web traffic occurs on a small portion of web sites like YouTube. Marketers are wise to post videos on YouTube to drive traffic rather than expecting videos to be found on their web sites.

can simply insert a hyperlink on their video to drive to an external web site, which is not exactly accurate.

Paid Ads. YouTube permits creators to put "annotation" text over their own videos, and create hyperlinks to other videos or a YouTube channel. However, advertisers must (as

Figure 4.3 There are strategies to increase conversion from a video to a web site; however, only a small percent of viewers leave a video immediately.

Figure 4.4   A General Electric "Healthymagination" advertisement appears in an "InVideo" format, which appears below a sponsored video.

of this writing) pay to have their web site's address appear over a video as a hyperlink (clickable). The advertisers have two choices, and one requires that they own the video.

- First, an advertiser can pay for a "pop-up" InVideo ad (see Figure 4.4), which can be purchased based on many factors such as content genre, region, keywords, and even specific channels. The InVideo ad, which is purchased by impressions not usually per click, can contain a message and a hyperlink.

- Another paid approach requires the advertiser to have its own video content and pay YouTube to promote the video based on keywords that are searched. First, the video creator selects his or her video, and chooses to "promote this video" to bid on ad space that appears with certain search-term results on YouTube. YouTube allows the video owner to set a bid price and a daily "cap" (maximum limit). After that, the creator can insert a simple "call to action" overlay advertisement (which includes text, a URL, and a small image). This will appear in lieu of an InVideo ad. Note that during this campaign, which can be turned off and on, the creator will not participate in advertising revenue of that video since another ad cannot appear.

- I have experimented with this video promotion tool by bidding small amounts (a tiny pennies) and only a tiny percent of people clicked the ad when it appeared, which is of little consequence since I pay only when they click. In my experiments, only about 2 percent of viewers clicked the URL. This did not appear to be a cost-effective option for me, since each person who clicked my ad would have to watch dozens of my videos before I recouped even pennies of what I paid to attract them. However, it's a remarkable ROI for the Amish shed manufacturer mentioned previously. Even if just one in hundreds of prospects follow Paul's path, the company has maintained an efficient customer acquisition cost given the high return ($10,000.00). This obviously doesn't work as nicely if a company is selling t-shirts or $20 software.

URL in Description. In lieu of a paid ad, the video description can contain an active hyperlink to your web site. It's important to include the entire URL (with *http://*) and place it early in the description so it's visible without a viewer needing to select "more" (see Figure 4.5 for an example). It's also helpful to have the URL appear in the video well before the ending, but not so early that the video appears overly promotional.

baldtruthradio — August 20, 2009 — http://www.thebaldtruth.com Kevin Nalty will be joining
Spencer Kobren this week 8/23/09 on The Bald Truth Radio...

Figure 4.5   Most of a YouTube video description is hidden, so URLs should appear early, but not before highly searched terms. Here are some valuable tips:

Compelling Call to Action. I have experimented with factors that increase the percentage of viewers who visit a site. Here are some valuable tips:

- The most compelling way to drive traffic to the site is additional video content by the same creator. For instance, if I direct viewers to "behind the scenes" or additional videos, I may see 4 to 10 percent of them visit.

- A campaign URL can also help. I knew it was unlikely that visitors of my Mr. Complicated video would visit a purchasing software web site, so I created a campaign site as www.MrComplicated.com (see Figure 4.6), which linked to my client, ClearPoint.

- A relevant discount or offer can also be effective. However, coupon code tracking will understate the performance of the campaign, as the traffic may not be immediate and the code may not be used.

Figure 4.6 One method of increasing conversion from a video to a web site is to provide a site or landing page that continues the entertainment experience.

- On a promotion for a cable television network's web site, I saw as high as 6 to 12 percent of the viewers visit the site. This was presumably because the videos were persuasive, and the destination site appealed to the audience.

Qualified Viewer. The more viral a video goes the smaller percent of people who will visit a URL. That's why qualified views are important. If the person found the video via search, and the video answers his question, then he is more likely to visit the destination web site. But if the video simply entertains him and flashes an irrelevant product, the viewer is likely to get on with his video session.

Three Types of Video for Businesses

By Daniel Sevitt

A former content leader at Metacafe, Daniel Sevitt now works at EyeView, and blogs about online video at the EyeView Digital Blog (http://blog.eyeviewdigital.com/).[1]

In identifying the different uses of video by business, it is helpful to look at the places these kinds of video can be found—embedded offsite, on the site's home page, and within the site. The careful placement of each video indicated different intent, which can be broken down into the following three types of video (see Figure 4.7):

Viral Video

Conversion Video

Educational Video

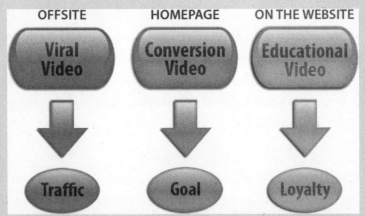

Figure 4.7 Videos have dramatically different roles based on locations. Marketers obsess on "viral" to capture customer attention, but many neglect video's role in educating, increasing sales conversion, improving service, or driving loyalty.

Viral Video

If online video got its first big break with the advent of YouTube, then viral video was the first breakout star for the medium. It's a classic case of business noticing what's going on in the real world and then trying hard to catch up.

Viral videos were the natural result of the culture of sharing that began once everyone you knew or did business with went online. Before there were viral videos, people shared jokes or inspirational PowerPoint presentations. The first viral videos were just evolved versions of the same.

As the demand for content grew, people started crafting video with one eye on making them go viral. There were several factors to consider. In order for a video to have a chance at becoming viral it needed to be most of the following:

- Original

- Unusual

- Unexpected

- Funny/mysterious/sexy

In addition, there was one more ingredient—a compound of timing, luck, and Internet serendipity—required for true online ubiquity. Almost impossible to fabricate, this elusive quality is still the thing that prevents most attempts at creating a viral video from succeeding. Nevertheless, businesses leapt at the chance to promote themselves through video, usually

(Continued)

by replicating a formula that had already achieved some success or notoriety.

Viral video differs from the other types of video in terms of its location. Viral video is at its best when it is found outside the company's site. Viral video is all about distribution and promotion. The company's aim is for the video to be embedded in many different sites to reach as wide an audience as possible. This is not always a good thing. Once a video can be embedded outside the company's site, the company loses control over the surrounding text and, perhaps more worrisome, the surrounding pictures and ads. If you allow your video to be watched anywhere, consider that viewers may see your logo and messaging juxtaposed with less savory images than what you would normally promote.

Metrics for Success. How do you measure the success of a viral video? It's not enough to consider the number of views only, although this is important. If you are looking at views, you need to decide "how much is enough?" The most popular videos on YouTube have been seen tens of millions of times. In order for your video to be considered a viral success, you might not need anywhere near those kinds of numbers. It depends who your products are targeting and whether or not you were noticed by the right kind of audience. If the video is hosted on a video-sharing site like YouTube, you might want to look at the number of comments your video receives to get an idea of the level of buzz you have created.

You can use a company like TubeMogul to upload and track your video across the Internet, but you probably need to combine that with your existing site analytics to judge whether or not it has an impact on your traffic. If you're aiming for a success metric that is even more intangible, such as brand building or buzz making, you will have to work out your own metric for success.

Creating a viral video is a bit like catching a fish . . . with your hands. It's slippery and almost impossible, but if you manage it, you'll feel fantastic.

Conversion Video

With all the uncertainty surrounding viral video, it seems much safer to manage video with more tangible goals. There are a number of reasons why site owners would want to place a video on their site. Video is a great way of engaging site visitors. *Engaged* visitors spend more time on web sites. More time spent on web sites means more opportunities to make money.

The most important thing for a commercial web site is to identify the goals of the site. As you build multiple points of entry to your site, you should carefully define the conversion goal for each. These are some of the most commonly seen conversion goals for commercial web sites:

- Enter Your Details—The aim of the site is to get visitors to give you contact details that can be used immediately or later to contact the customer and initiate business.

- Download This File—Installing the file may be the first stage in turning the site visitor into a customer.

(Continued)

- Buy This Product—A direct inducement to the site visitor to pay money in return for a product or service.

- Deposit Now—Used by companies to establish the financial relationship that turns browsers into committed customers.

Once you have a clear conversion goal for your landing page, a good conversion video should focus on driving users to that goal. Video does that in a number of ways. To begin with, a conversion video, like any other kind of video, should be an engaging experience drawing viewers in and helping them to spend more time on the site. A successful conversion video should carry a clear call to action. This can be part of the script, part of the visual, part of the player, or any combination of the three. The call to action in the video must be aligned with the conversion goal for the page the video sits in to ensure that there is a clear path for the viewer to follow.

A brief review of the available material on the Internet throws up an abundance of lists of tips for making your corporate video. If you have questions about any aspect of video making, from the perfect duration to the perfect volume, you will find someone with an opinion on the subject. The best thing you can do is to start with what you think makes sense and to test it on your site.

But before you can test the effectiveness of your video, you need to make sure people are watching. There are many ways to promote the viewing of your video on your site. Once you have produced a video that you are happy with, you owe it to yourself to exploit as many of these methods as you can. First of all, you want to ensure that people can find your video. Make it visible and accessible. If the video is a key part of your conversion strategy for a page, then make sure people know where it is. Once you are happy with its location on the page, you should consider having the video *autoplay* (start automatically when a visitor comes to your page). If autoplay seems too aggressive, there are variations you can try such as having the video autoplay without sound (but with subtitles) until the viewer opts in to listening as well as watching.

Metrics for Success. If the goal for your conversion video is to increase conversions, then the metric for success should be easy. When the number, or the percentage, of your conversions rises, then the video is a success. Depending on the conversion goal, increased conversion can have a direct impact on the revenues of your company. It is no wonder that more and more companies are focusing on conversion video as the most likely to provide a return on their investment.

Educational Video

Educational video probably doesn't sit on your home page. There are a number of reasons for adding educational videos to your site and, unlike viral and conversion videos, your educational video can help you achieve multiple goals without detracting from the video's success. That means your educational video doesn't have to be quite as tightly focused on a single goal. With educational video, you have the freedom to build toward a number of achievements.

(*Continued*)

Primarily, an educational video is there to educate. But, educational video can also help to establish trust and thought-leadership. Visitors to your site who move beyond the landing page and begin to delve deeper into everything your site has to offer may be looking for more information. We know that video is an excellent medium for distilling information, and inquiring visitors can find much to satisfy their curiosity in a well-made video.

Good video can be a real differentiator for your company against your competitors. You can use the videos to do things that other people in your market are failing to do well. If a visitor learns everything he needs from you, he's more likely to come back when he's ready to become a consumer.

Educational video can also take the strain away from your customer support team. Linking your videos to a FAQs document or any other part of your online support can help answer some of the questions and pain points that would otherwise make their way to a customer representative. The interaction can often be even more satisfying with the customers feeling they were able to get the answer they wanted in a format with which they are at ease.

Educational videos can guide viewers through a difficult process and help to ease the concerns of nervous browsers. They can help to build a mentor-mentee relationship between the site and its visitors, which may have a positive impact.

There are fewer restrictions in educational video in terms of duration and messaging. It's probably not smart to load your educational videos with sales messaging, but beyond that there is a freedom to communicate clearly knowing that anyone watching is doing so with less enticement than other forms of video.

Metrics for Success. Educational video may be one of the hardest types of video to manage in terms of ROI. The production costs are as high as other forms of video, but the number of views should not measure success. There are other metrics that should be captured, such as "time spent on video" or how many chapters of your video were viewed. Not every player will provide you with this kind of data, but it can be invaluable for establishing ROI.

Educational videos are less likely to be promoted than other kinds of videos. They are more correctly positioned and targeted to specific customers at different stages in the sales cycle. Educational videos are designed to prevent customer confusion and deliver clarity.

If your educational video is aimed at reducing the number of referrals to customer support, then a clear reduction is the best measure of success. Beyond that tangible proof, the success of educational videos is notoriously difficult to determine.

Once you are committed to making video part of your corporate marketing strategy, there are still a number of questions to be asked. Choosing which kind of video you want to produce may depend on how you measure the return on your marketing spend. There are risks and rewards for each kind of video, but there is no denying the potential impact of the medium. Harnessing that impact and using it to your advantage is one of the key challenges facing online marketers today.

Some Additional Considerations

- It is rare for me to find such an insightful framework for looking at the various marketing goals for online video across various stages of the customer funnel. As marketers, we often obsess with the top of the sales funnel and neglect holes along the bottom. I liked this framework even before I realized it was written by Daniel Sevitt, who coincidentally approached me in 2006 to feature my videos on Metacafe.

- Many brands can benefit from awareness alone. Television ads very rarely lead to immediate purchase, and most brands can be marketed without dragging someone to a product.com web site. How many products do you own that you purchased without visiting a manufacturer's web site?

- Note that it's ideal for businesses to create a custom video for important audiences and common tasks they seek to complete. The video will work more effectively if it relates to search terms (which will tell you if a customer is exploring a category or ready to buy) or is customized to a site's context.

- Many companies have loads of engaging, informative, and persuasive content. They use videos internally or with salespeople, but haven't posted them on the company's web site, much less on sites like YouTube. So search engines can't possibly find them, nor can prospects.

- While you're trying to find a way to go viral or engage audiences in entertaining ways, at least post your promotional or educational content on your site and

YouTube. Unless the videos are archaic or poor, they can't do harm and could help customers find you.

Video and Corporate Communication

Before I left Johnson & Johnson (J&J), there was a new word I began hearing in the public relations circles. It used to be all about *transparency*, but then the word *dissintermediate* started to surface. J&J didn't just have a credo hanging on a wall that gave lip service to patients, physicians, nurses, employees, and shareholders. The credo was spoken of frequently, and truly guided decisions—in the same way that other companies are driven deeply by profit, innovation, competition, legal fear, growth, or cost cutting.

Anyway, dissintermediate was the term designed to ensure that the media didn't shape J&J's reputation entirely. In a crisis, from the Tylenol tampering of the 1980s to BP's handling of the Deepwater Horizon oil spill, the media sometimes becomes both a feeder and follower of public opinion. Truth dissipates in McCarthy-like witch hunts of companies (Enron, the banking industry) or people ("Octomom," Michael Jackson). The reporter knows the public vilifies individuals, so the journalist's story (despite an attempt for objectivity) naturally feeds the public sentiment—or else the public resents the reporter.

Consider how JetBlue and Domino's used YouTube to help damage control in the face of difficult situations, and the positive press that resulted from approaching a crisis head-on through YouTube.

CEOs once took out full-page ads to address the public after, for example, an accident (Exxon Valdez, product recall, or an airplane crash). Now, company leaders can address people directly, unedited and unmediated. If the public is so inclined, anyone can become his own reporter. This individual can assess the message and decide if the company is sincere, well intentioned, honest, transparent, and apologetic—or not. And with video, that opinion will be less about packaged news sound bites and more about how the CEO comes across in longer-form video.

Ronald Reagan mastered politics because he knew how to perform for television. Today's CEOs won't live or die by their video to the public, but those who hide behind public-relations machines and reporters (instead of speaking to people directly) will be ceding their fate to potentially less capable or interested parties.

The CEOs who understand how to talk into a camera lens—as if they're looking into the eyes of a friend—will be at a significant advantage. The ones who resist overproducing the message with graphics, a fancy set, and lighting will likely appear more accessible and sincere.

CHAPTER 5

The Most Visceral Form of Social Media

This book is part of the "New Rules of Social Media" series, and it is impossible to explore online video comprehensively without acknowledging its significant social currency. In this chapter, you will learn:

- How online video remains a social medium despite the increase of professional content.

- Why those viewing online video as a distribution channel often fail.

- How online video offers marketers a more visceral, natural, and sustainable opportunity than some of the popular and fleeting social-media sites.

Discovering Community: The Backbone of Online Video

Many marketers consider online video as another distribution for promotional messaging, or see it as a chance to go viral. However, at the core of today's online video is a vibrant community of people. Consider the following:

- For years, YouTube viewers have formed their own grassroots meet-ups across the globe. Some are formal events attended by hundreds and thousands of people, while others are just a few dozen people meeting spontaneously.

- The regular viewers of YouTube interact virtually and in person, and most of the top 100 most-subscribed people are at most two degrees of separation from one another (I can almost always find someone who personally knows another video creator).

- Numerous YouTube personalities have started romantic relationships with their fellow creators. I can think of two high-profile marriages that would not have occurred without this medium.

As an introvert, I was not drawn to online video to make virtual friends. I simply wanted people to see my videos, and perhaps make some money from advertisements. I share my early experience with online video to help you understand this vital element that is inextricably linked to online video.

My False Start. It took me nearly a year to appreciate the social aspect of online video, and my personal account may help you expedite your own understanding. I spent nine months distributing my videos through a variety of online-video web sites late in 2005 and was thrilled if 100 people watched. Now, that occurs within seconds after I hit "submit." My most profound discovery about online video came in mid-2006 when I discovered, quite accidentally, that online-video views were dependent on community participation. People on YouTube were commenting on my videos, sharing them, and even making video replies. A few individuals became my early advocates, and I still regard them as I do my freshman roommates. Time pulls you apart, but there's an affinity that lasts.

When I began to interact with my audience and other online-video creators, I quickly became one of the most-viewed creators. News reporters often ask me why I began making online videos, and the reality is that I've been making short comedy videos since I was young. The simple truth is that I just wanted an audience and perhaps some residual income. Again, I did not post videos to make new friends or become a star. My wife and I were in for a surprise.

Oh, Dear. Fans? Quite suddenly, in 2006, I found a vibrant community forming around my videos. They were virtual friends who promoted me passionately, gave me feedback, collaborated with me, and responded to my videos with comments and videos. I began collaborating with local YouTubers to make videos and found it scary, but fascinating, to meet strangers based on a common passion.

Before long, I had a regular base of viewers. They created a Wikipedia page for me, developed virtual fan clubs, and rallied around "Nalts," a college nickname I stole from my brother (he's a priest now, so he has forgiven me). I was flattered and terrified to become a public figure, and worked hard to convince people that I was not Kevin Nalty, but "Kevin Nalts." I blocked my phone number, feared for my kids, and worked hard to obscure my residence.

Hooked on Community. But the fear was overcome by the passion that came with collaborating with fellow creators. Suddenly, I was invited into *collabs*, which is YouTube shorthand for developing a video together. After a few,

I was hooked. I reached out to my favorite online-video creators, and began a series of these. One of the individuals was a popular YouTube personality named Christine Gambito (known online as "HappySlip" and pictured in Figure 5.1). I met her in her home in New York City, and she came up with an idea that exponentially grew my audience. I pretended to sneak into her apartment and get caught by her in the process. She drew attention to my video, and my "subscriber" numbers jolted overnight. To the audience, it was like watching Samantha from *Bewitched* appear on *Happy Days*. Later, one of YouTube's most popular personalities, Renetto, agreed to meet me in Baltimore and give me a Renetto makeover by shaving my head. I became the poster

Figure 5.1 Online video stars often help jumpstart others. Christine Gambito, known as HappySlip, introduced the author to her vibrant audience.

child for collaborations, and as a result each creator would inherit a significant portion of the other's audience. I would later fly to Los Angeles to appear in an HBO series (*Hooking Up*) starring YouTubers, as well as in an episode of "The Retarded Policeman" with producer Greg Benson, who ran Mediocrefilms, one of the most-subscribed channels today.

Physical Community

Physical gatherings are also tangible proof of the cultlike following of YouTube. When I helped promote a YouTube gathering in New York City on July 7, 2007 (see Figure 5.2), hundreds of viewers attended, and many (in quite surreal moments) asked me for autographs. People had traveled across the globe to meet fellow YouTube creators and

One YouTuber in NYC

Figure 5.2 As proof of social nature of online video, the author's February 2007 video announced a New York City YouTube gathering on July 7, 2007. One of the first "YouTube Gatherings," it attracted hundreds of people from the United States and beyond to meet fellow webstars and viewers.

viewers. One brought his daughter and asked me to autograph a banana (after viewing a video called "Banana Man" that I had made with my son). It was both intoxicating and strangely exhausting. Today, when I attend these gatherings, I am still mobbed. But I am relieved to find hotter and more current webstars getting more attention.

YouTube has sponsored only one live public event (YouTube Live, November 2008). But dozens of well-attended events—organized and promoted by YouTube community members in a grassroot style—have occurred in large cities, including Atlanta, San Francisco, New York, London, and Chicago.

Video Trumps Social Media

Most marketers are pursuing customers via such popular social-media sites as Facebook and Twitter, but I believe online video is better for marketers for a variety of reasons. I have proposed this at marketing conferences and in trade publications, and it is often the source of interesting debate. Consider the following:

- Online video outranks many online activities (see Figure 5.3), and more Internet users (62 percent) watch video than use social-networking sites (46 percent).[1]

- YouTube is the second-largest search engine, and its use has grown exponentially (doubling from 2006 to 2009).[2]

- Video provides more performance data (we marketers can track how long people watch a video, for instance, but have little data about how many individuals read "tweets" on Twitter). Facebook provides minimal

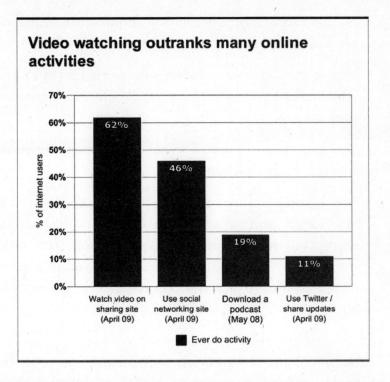

Figure 5.3 Video watching outranks many online activities.
Source: Pew Internet & American Life Project survey conducted March 26–April 29, 2009. Based on all adult Internet users $n = 1,687$, with a margin of error of $+/-3$ percent. Data on podcast downloading comes from a Pew Internet & American Life Project survey conducted April 8–May 11, 2008. Based on all adult Internet users $n = 1,153$, with a margin of error of $+/-3$ percent.

metrics on page views, although some advertisers have inserted their own tracking software.

- People tend to notice advertisements when they're engaged in a passive online-viewing state rather than immersed in social dialogue with friends.

- Video is simply more visceral than text or ads. If a picture is worth a thousand words, a video is worth exponentially more. In general, multimedia helps people learn and retain information more effectively.[3]

- You've got a chance at being seen—organically and via paid media. Facebook, to me, seems more cluttered and overwhelming.

- You can control your message more easily, especially through branded channels.

- Finally, online video is more likely to be discovered via Google and other search engines. Although the search engines are increasingly indexing "real time" information like Twitter, video is currently a more effective way to get your message seen via relevant searches.

Facebook and Twitter are indisputably popular, but where does a brand come into play? Do people really want to "friend" a brand? Maybe if it's one they already love, but that's not a good customer acquisition play; it's more of a retention strategy.

Twitter is good for promotion of content providers, stars, and bloggers (who often report Twitter as their most significant source of traffic). But there are not as many opportunities for advertising, and I'm fundamentally opposed to people getting paid to tweet about a company (especially since there's generally not enough room to disclose the fact). I am frustrated by spam that promises I can earn cash per tweet, as I would unlikely "follow" someone who was promoting too frequently.

Perhaps a brand should advertise on Facebook, but many brands create their own Facebook presence without a content strategy. Unless the brand already has an active base of enthusiasts (like Coke), it's unlikely that individuals would "fan" it.

Facebook and Twitter are conversations between people, and advertising is an interruption. YouTube is somewhere people visit both to socialize and casually graze videos, so a visceral ad will catch your attention if the video is boring. Promotions within a video (sponsorships) are much better because they're contextually relevant, entertaining, and there are implied endorsements.

A Pew study showed that 62 percent of U.S. Internet users have watched online video, and only 46 percent have engaged in social media. Ninety percent of young adults use video-sharing sites.[4]

Naturally, there are loads of questions we might ask about this data: There's a big difference between "did it once" and "do it daily," and I'm not even sure some social-media users *know* they're using social media. Online-video viewers are more likely to know they're watching online video. Of course, brands need to consider both online video and social media as being exponentially more influential than interruption advertising.

YouTube is (at its core) a social-media site that uses the most visceral form of social media: video. It began as a community of creators and audiences, and many "in real life" (IRL) relationships have formed via the web site.

But it has two advantages beyond other social media (Facebook, Twitter, etc.). First, it's easier to access: You don't need to register, create a profile, or be a hardcore social-media nut to "pop in" for a quick engaging video. Second, video has value to people who have absolutely no interest in the social aspects of the medium. Some simply want to engage in online recreation or watch a few funny clips.

By contrast to social media, consider what video offers:

- It requires no routine checking, registration, intrusion, or self-exposure.

- People can watch a video, and go away—it's low maintenance, easy for even the technologically phobic, and attractive even if you're shy.

- It tends to be more engaging and influential because in addition to the social aspects, you can discover all sorts of niche content.

- There is a wider marketplace for online video's applications, making it significantly broader than social media's reach. Eventually, every baby boomer will have seen an online video, but how many will spend time each day checking Facebook?

So I contend, although I am disputed on this matter, that online video will always trump social media. It has a lower barrier to entry and it's easier to sustain use. Many people start social-networking accounts with great vision, and then abandon them soon after, hence the term *twitter fatigue*. Nielsen reports that 60 percent of Twitter users fail to return again, and having 50,000 followers means quite little if most of those people forgot Twitter exists. This is true for Facebook and other sites. You either become obsessive-compulsive with it, or you ditch it completely.

The average blogger has the lifespan of a fruit fly. Generally, for every person who contributes to social media, there are maybe 100 that consume it but stay quiet. Approximately 1 in 100 of my viewers comment, for instance. I am not arguing that blogs aren't important for creators and readers, however, and video channels also have abandonment rates.

Social media is important to marketers because it's where customers are influencing each other in ways brands can finally measure and engage. My hypothesis, however, is that while social media will continue to become part of our lives, it will lose much of its charm in years ahead. People will discover that obsessing with social media can be as counterproductive to productivity as spending a workday managing an e-mail box. Brands will discover that social media is one answer, but not the answer to marketing and communications. Perhaps in the coming years, the term *social media* will feel as clichéd as I hope *viral video* becomes. The notion of a brand having a social media strategy will seem as silly as having an e-business strategy.

In the end, all of these mediums and tactics are in service of a marketing strategy, not strategies alone. If you are a vice president of e-business or social media, I'd argue you are either a technologist, public relations person, or marketer in disguise.

CHAPTER 6
Inside YouTube

In this chapter, you will learn:

- Why YouTube is so critical to an online-video strategy.

- The least a marketer needs to know about YouTube without reading an entire book about it, or spending hours each day engaged in it (sadly, like the author).

- Insights can bring you from "I know it's an important web site" to "I'm more savvy than 80 percent of the average users".

- Tips and tricks for helping you market more effectively and avoid being lost in the overwhelming clutter.

YouTube 101

When I speak at corporations or marketing conferences, I often poll audiences about their YouTube IQ. I find it alarming that few marketers have even heard of YouTube stars with larger and more vibrant audiences than many well-known television shows. I recently surveyed conference attendees via a smartphone poll, and discovered that 60 percent of the marketers visited YouTube only when

Who Is the YouTube User?

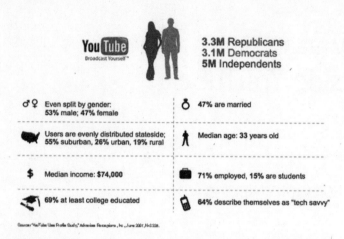

Figure 6.1 Who is the YouTube user? (YouTube fact sheet and advertiser perceptions study.)

Source: www.youtube.com/t/fact_sheet

Source: http://elitestv.com/pub/2009/07/youtube-demographics-round-up.

someone sent them a link via e-mail. I doubt we would see as many television or print advertisements if marketers didn't watch television or buy magazines.

Fortunately, many executives have teenagers, who are unavoidable reminders that media-consumption patterns are changing, and the time we spend on both the mobile Web and online video is surpassing traditional e-mail.

According to a YouTube fact sheet,[1] (see Figure 6.1) the user base is broad in age range (18 to 55), evenly divided between males and females, and spans all geographies. Fifty-one percent of users go to YouTube weekly or more often, and 52 percent of 18- to 34-year-olds share videos often with friends and colleagues.

YouTube reports that its audience is 53 percent male and 47 percent female. Fifty-five percent are urban with a median income of $74,000 per year. Nearly 70 percent are college educated, 47 percent are married, the median age is 33, and 71 percent are employed.

I am almost embarrassed to admit that a decade ago, I provided executives with an Internet 101 session to help them understand its importance. Now, there's a burgeoning need for a YouTube 101 course to help marketers understand the platform, see how leading brands are using it, and consider the implications on a marketing mix.

I could no more read a book about how to use YouTube than an instruction manual for e-mail or a phone system, so I'll assume you, too, want "just the facts."

A Marketer's "Cheat Sheet" on YouTube

Like many portals or social-media sites, YouTube can appear overwhelming at first glance. But you need only to know some basics to understand your marketing options (and perhaps proactively find content that you will personally enjoy).

Creating an account. In minutes, you can set up your own YouTube account (which now requires you to create a Google account). You can remain anonymous by picking a username that is obscure, and requesting that YouTube make it impossible for others to find your account via your e-mail address). By default, YouTube will alert you via e-mail more often than you may prefer. So you may want to limit these messages to specific events.

Search for your brand. Since YouTube is the number two search engine after Google, you may wish to search keywords or terms that your target customers may use. Will they find you, a competitor, or a consumer-generated video that casts your brand or company in a negative light? It's also worth searching for your own brand and a few competitors' brands, and including general market terms. Don't worry if you don't like what you discover, because this book will identify ways to increase the odds that your videos rank highly. Failing that, you can bid on terms and promote your video, similar to the way brands advertise on Google.

Create a free monitoring service. YouTube offers the ability for you to "subscribe" to keywords, which effectively provides you with a free monitoring tool. For example, you can subscribe to your brand name, company name, competitors, or general terms important to your marketplace.

Making YouTube matter to you. Your gestalt of YouTube is probably driven from the YouTube videos you've seen televised or the few you've seen online. However, it's helpful for a marketer to rediscover YouTube by pursuing videos related to a personal hobby or passion. I encourage people to relearn YouTube by searching for content of interest: travel, sports, music, how-to, or any hobby. When you search for videos, you can conduct an advanced search to refine the search in various ways (by time period, total views, viewer ratings, etc.). If you find a channel or video creator that appeals to you, select the orange "subscribe" button. Like receiving a magazine subscription or a DVR series or a season pass, you will be alerted to new videos by that individual when you visit your subscription page.

Surf popular content. YouTube offers a number of different ways to identify content without searching, and a "videos" tab can take you to the most-viewed or most-popular videos (based on ratings, comments, duration of average view, and other factors). You can also search "channels" to learn what content creators are the most subscribed or most viewed (see Figure 6.2). Note that you can set the parameters to reflect "all time" or within the past month,

Figure 6.2 It's important to see what videos are popular or most viewed. To see these, select "Videos," then narrow search by genre or time period (weekly, monthly).

week, or day. I usually encourage brands to peruse the top 100 most-popular videos of the week or month. Unless you represent your target audience, it's not important for you to like these videos. These creators and channels are what *viewers* like. While some brands have legitimate taste and tone concerns about where their marketing appears, avoid the mistake of critiquing the content. What matters most is the audience, and whether it is consistent with your target.

Engage if you dare. I suspect that few marketers will dive into the fish tank of YouTube, but I find this vital to understanding the medium. As an example, I learned a lot about how to influence bloggers when I began blogging. I was able to see through the smoke and mirrors of paid search when I executed my own search campaign. And I've learned more about marketing via YouTube by creating and watching than I could have ever learned from trade magazines. If you're inclined, shoot some video (using one of the many simple and affordable video cameras like those popularized by Flip). You will soon realize how hard it is to get views initially, and why partnering with well-viewed creators and channels is so important. If you are camera shy, try simply commenting on a video, rating it, favoriting it, or even messaging the creator.

YouTube Secrets

I am very careful to *not* reveal confidential information that I have learned from Google employees, or through off-the-record conversations with industry colleagues or creators. But some secrets of YouTube have become public, and YouTube has created multiple blogs to dispel myths and clarify issues.

YouTube and Money. YouTube monetizes a small minority of its content. By that, I mean it generates advertising revenue surrounding videos that it shares with the content creators. Many journalists and analysts have speculated on the percent of YouTube videos that are monetized, and have varied from 3 to 15 percent in their projections. These figures can be misleading, of course, since monetizing could mean low-cost banners or robust sponsorships with higher-impact and more expensive ad units. What people really want to know is: (1) whether YouTube is profitable, and (2) how much money content creators and YouTube stars make.

Why Google Is Hush on YouTube Revenue and Profit. Google is notoriously quiet, and rarely releases information about YouTube's financial status. This is a constant source of frustration among journalists; however, there is little upside for YouTube to disclose financials. If profit is down, it will negatively influence YouTube's relationships with content and media partners, and undermine its efforts with advertisers. If it is startling positive, it will draw interest from copyright attorneys and rally competitors. Even the most aggressive estimates of today's YouTube revenue represent a very small portion of Google's annual revenue. So why did Google pay $1.6 billion for YouTube, accept some interim profit loss, and assume liability of copyright infringement? The simple answer is that Google's focus is on anticipating technology needs before they are evident. Google is tolerating short-term pain to invest in a future where video consumption will be driven by search.

I do remain perplexed by YouTube's persistent reluctance to share specific case studies on the performance of advertising. The company has worked with brands to analyze data and conduct recall surveys, but has published precious little. The "party line" is that the data is client privileged, but it makes many wonder if the data substantiates the impact of campaigns.

Algorithms Squashed the Editors. Almost nothing you see on YouTube is by accident—or by an editor anymore. While YouTube editors arguably once possessed more power than most network executives (creating instant celebrities by featuring them on the home page), the model is now driven primarily by relevance and economics. YouTube allows content creators and advertisers to promote their videos for a fee, in a variety of ways that are both obvious and subtle. Editors continue to serve some role in selecting spotlight videos (which are featured on the home page, category pages, and "featured videos" lists surrounding other videos). I've parodied this fact in my low-budget cartoon (see Figure 6.3).

The role of the YouTube editor, who once controlled the destiny of amateurs, has diminished. YouTube still plays favorites, and especially for important content creators and television shows or films. More recently, YouTube has put increasing emphasis on the new establishment of studios

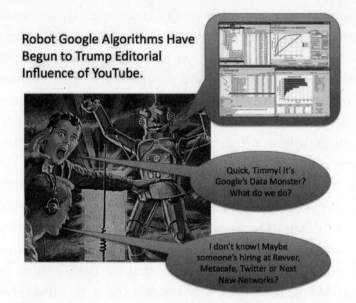

Figure 6.3 A cartoon parody I use to illustrate the declining role of the YouTube editor. Videos are now primarily driven by algorithms informed by user behavior and preference.

developing less expensive shows and series specifically for online video (versus television).

The Chain Reaction. A visit to YouTube often can result in a chain reaction. Viewers begin to watch one video, and several related videos draw them deeper. The video-sharing site, Metacafe, was once the master of prompting addictive viewing sessions. Now, YouTube is drawing upon its data-oriented parent, Google, to facilitate what I call the "video roach motel" model. For example, there are a series of humorous videos with children giggling or doing and saying funny things. People have viewed these videos in one session, and if they like one they tend to like another. As a result, these videos are woven together via related videos, and are viewed hundreds of millions of times.

Amazon's Recommendation Model. If you've purchased a book on Amazon, you may notice the site promotes related books purchased by people with similar preferences. Similarly, YouTube has learned from the billions of views, and it attempts to provide videos based on a viewer's stated preference or past behavior. I have not found YouTube's recommendations to be accurate, but I have found related videos to be relevant.

Cheating is Less Effective. When my video, "Farting in Public," was featured by YouTube, I noticed some savvy creators and advertisers were tagging their videos with terms identical to the ones attached to my video. As a result, their videos appeared beside my videos, and that increased their views. Many people continue to post their videos as a "video reply" to my most-viewed videos in hopes of driving their views. Over time, this gaming has lost its impact because YouTube's related videos are driven by factors that individuals can manipulate less easily, such as aggregated viewer behavior. If YouTube discovers that certain people prefer similar video creators (and their viewing patterns and ratings correlate), then that informs the related videos that appear and gain additional views. For example, if people enjoy my sophomoric pranks, we'd expect to see similar prank videos appear after my videos play. Likewise, if people enjoy my family-friendly moments, they may be presented with those videos of Shay Butler (ShayCarl/Shaytards), a fellow father documenting his absurd family moments.

YouTube Is Hungry. Google has always minimized mass-market display ads in lieu of relevant text advertisements. It was the first search engine to abandon the lucrative profit of banner ads on its home page. But YouTube has shown its desire for revenue by accepting significant homepage takeovers, in which television and film ads represent the majority of the area above the fold (the portion of a Web page that appears on a typical Web browser without requiring a person to scroll down). This is common on sites like Microsoft, Yahoo!, and AOL, but very atypical of a Google property. These programs negatively impact a user's experience, but command larger advertising spends. So the decision to permit dramatic takeovers can only suggest that Google is trying to offset the high infrastructure costs of streaming the majority of videos that lack advertising.

"The Secret Sauce" of Google/YouTube

As I have mentioned, video content will rise or fall based on consumer relevance (duration of view, relevance by keyword, ratings, view counts, favorites, etc.), but the most vital aspects are black box, or confidential. We can make some solid deductions and predictions when we consider the algorithms that drive Google's rankings (how certain Web pages appear on the first page for certain keyword searches).

Google's search results reward advertisers who bid high prices for paid placement, and organic (natural) results based on whether the content is relevant (as defined by inbound links and whether we engage, or return to Google to refine the search).

Not surprisingly, YouTube is replicating that Google model—giving love to content that either satisfied viewers or can be monetized via the Partners program. Unfortunately, YouTube is less transparent about whether a video receives primacy because of relevance or ad dollars. There isn't a clear visual divide between paid and organic videos, even though the new labels (spotlight, promoted, featured) are a step in that direction, and this will continue to become more clear to even the naive online surfer, who still can't distinguish between an ad and an organic result on Google.

The "secret sauce" is Google's proprietary scheme for keeping the viewers engaged, and ensuring that the content continues to not just satisfy their curiosity, but more important, hook them for more viewing (and it works based on average views consumed by a YouTuber relative to a Yahoo! Video viewer). The secret sauce is, and will always remain, highly confidential and in flux. Otherwise, we'll game the system through various tricks: The algorithm that makes up that sauce will get smarter and more difficult to fool.

We can complain about the secret sauce, or accept it and evolve. That means our video content needs to be relevant and captivating. Partners have a distinct advantage, because YouTube would be foolish to favor videos it can't monetize (derive income for YouTube and its Partners by advertising). So we'll see powerful and deep-pocketed commercial networks and producers (and advertisers) get an increasing leg up on amateurs by giving YouTube a financial incentive to show their videos love and attention through paid buys and favored placement. These entities can pay for love, or YouTube may give them free love to hook new audiences and mutually monetize their content long term. Backed by a Pepsi sponsorship, PopTub, a quirky series featuring topical YouTube videos, initially had premium placement across YouTube. And sometimes amateurs get lucky because their content gets stuck on the home page (YouTube employees confided that technical errors provided advantages to some Partners).

In the meantime, here are some basic tips, and some haven't changed since last year when I wrote my free e-book ("How to Become Popular on YouTube Without Any Talent").

1. Create videos about content that is topical and searched. That's how YouTube Partners Michael Buckley (WhatTheBuckShow) and Phil DeFranco (Sxephil) attracted a following that is now somewhat self-sustaining. Their daily videos provide commentary on recent news, and as a result are widely accessed through YouTube search.

2. Build a distinct niche, and market your videos via similar creators and properties (blogs) beyond YouTube.

3. Continue to reply to videos that are already popular. The viewer will see the thumbnail, and your video will pick up "spillover."

4. Ensure the videos are tagged appropriately, but are also compelling and engage the viewer. Otherwise, algorithms will mistake those for spam. It doesn't work anymore to tag your video with *sex* and expect that video to sail.

5. Those thumbnails (images that represent a video) are as vital as anything. If a video is promoted, featured, or spotlighted, the viewer will decide to engage based on the title, thumbnail, and duration (we still want short videos).

6. A secret tip: Leave a few moments of blank space after your video, so your viewers are less likely to escape via related videos served involuntarily by YouTube after the video plays (you want your viewer instead choosing a thumbnail for your own video, and those appear beneath the video). Many creators now *tease* their other videos at the end of each video.

7. Finally, you'd better monetize your videos and become a YouTube Partner. Sponsored videos that aren't monetized are not likely to thrive as well as entertaining videos that earn Google and its Partners ad dollars.

It is indeed harder to become an overnight success, especially when we have a vicious cycle of fame: It takes lots of views to qualify as a Partner, and it takes Partner status to get more views. So the rich may get richer, and the bar is rising. But don't despair! JeepersMedia is surpassing 100,000 subscribers, and had only 4,300 subscribers 10 months ago. There's still room for new video creators who tap distinct audience niches and manage (like Jeepers) to rank continually among the most highly rated videos of the day.

And as long as the subscription model remains important to new YouTube addicts, your success breeds success. A good video can prompt a new YouTube user to subscribe (especially if the creator asks or reminds him to), and then your chances of that individual watching your future videos are much higher.

CHAPTER 7
Agencies Searching for Role

In this chapter, you will learn:

- How marketing, strategy, Internet, and advertising agencies are adapting to the emergence of online video and social media.

- How to predict some of the behaviors these companies will exhibit based on their response to the emergence of the Internet as a marketing channel.

- How to improve your investment in online video based on the successes and failures of large campaigns.

Learning from the Past

When consumer preferences for media change quickly, marketing and advertising agencies exhibit three different behaviors: (1) denial, (2) hastened exuberance, or (3) gradual evolution. When I speak to agencies, I liken the rise of online video and social media to the arrival of Internet advertising. Web advertising (banners, web sites, paid search) had similar ramifications to the agency landscape to the arrival of Twitter, Facebook, and YouTube. The world's largest brands depend on the advice and execution of several large agency holding companies, which generally operate via loosely affiliated specialty companies.

Similarly, at the millennium's onset, many of these individual companies or holding companies employed one or more e-business experts. What these subject-matter experts possessed in Internet knowledge, however, they lacked in influence or direct client access. The power in agencies is generally relegated to the agency's founders, creative leaders, rainmakers (sales leaders), or those overseeing the agency's top accounts. Individual subject-matter experts can't possibly be fluent on each client's strategy or marketplace, and may provide conflicting advice or overwhelm a client. As a result, we marketers have demanded the agency to assign one person or small team for our primary interface. Ultimately, the e-business experts, like today's experts in social media or online video, failed to have significant impact. As a result, agency executives began to acquire or incubate Internet agencies, working to balance often-competing agendas: building an empowered collection of subject-matter experts while maintaining a primary emphasis on the unique needs of clients. This is the reason I have chosen to consult independently rather than become an agency's online-video monkey. Still, I have some tips for agencies as they engage in online video and social media.

How Agencies Can Engage in Social Media

1. 101 Course for Every Department. Everyone at a traditional agency should have a basic understanding of the Internet, as well as a basic understanding of new forms of media. Not everyone needs to Twitter, but they should be able to describe a successful case study related to each major media form (Twitter, Facebook, YouTube, Digg, and whatever else comes along). They may discover that social media can help their department instead of threaten its existence.

2. Enlist Senior Champion. Agencies generally need a senior advocate for innovative new solutions that might otherwise lack attention or fail. The champion's role is to focus the attention of the cross-agency groups, and determine how the holding company or affiliates will evolve to pursue new channels and adapt to consumer-behavior changes. Is it wise to embed specialists in each division or account team, or to centralize expertise? Should the media department handle social media, or does it fit better in a strategy, research, or planning division? The answers to these two questions alone result in fundamental implications and trade-offs.

3. Take Small Innovation Team Off Billable Clock. Someone or a small team should be relieved of the typical billable-hour pressure to identify and explore emerging mediums. While some changes may not yet offer the agency a profit model, they often can help a client reach its goals. This person or team can share best practices, and identify what partners, vendors, and consultants can solve various problems. In some cases, they can simply educate account teams and connect them with these experts. An agency's first experiment with a time-consuming project might have this team "run point" to manage a client project—from linking tactics to a client's strategy to collecting relevant metrics. In many cases, the agency should educate account teams (and not just those pitching a new assignment), hand the project over, and return to collect the performance metrics—ensuring it's not redundant to other departments. Some of this work may have already been done on billable time, but if it's buried inside an account team, it's not going to help the new pitch or other client.

4. Partnering with External Specialists. Niche social-media players (start-ups and specialty firms) and larger agencies can often help an agency accelerate learning. This is a sensible move by agencies that do not yet have sufficient demand for hiring full-time specialists, but have clients expecting the expertise. However, agency profitability depends on keeping full-time employees billable and minimizing external expenses. For specialists and agencies to partner in a mutually beneficial way, it's not enough to have an aligned focus on a client's outcome. Both the specialty vendor and the lead agency (usually the firm with an existing client relationship) need clear roles and mutual profitability. If a Twitter guru can offer guidance, this person will want a seat at the table from the start, as well as clearly defined boundaries. The specialist's early input may help optimize a program, kill it justifiably, or save it from becoming an embarrassing case study in industry news. Conceptually, this is simple, but I've seen it at its best and worst. For example, my "agency of record" once seamlessly introduced a social-media guru who had been well informed of my marketplace and brand. I didn't even realize he was an outside consultant until I saw his e-mail address. This was refreshing after a less positive example; my digital agency once engaged a consultant to provide expertise on technology integration, and his ego, poor listening skills, and lack of industry knowledge was irritating. I had to ask the agency to remove him from our account. Likewise, agencies face temptations to round out expertise that would be better left to specialists. For instance, if a leading social-media monitoring tool is better than the agency's homegrown web-monitoring solution, then the agency might be wise to outsource this function and mark it up (for adding value, configuring the tool, and analyzing the results).

5. Balancing Rogue Specialists and Protective Agencies. Social-media start-ups (and especially consultants) are sometimes brilliant solo players, but not instinctive jazz ensemble performers. The latter is required to sustain comprehensive agency services. Other specialists simply prefer a specific niche, and have no interest in services beyond their realm of passion. The latter tend to provide subject-matter expertise that complements rather than threatens the agency-client relationship.

The failure of partnerships—between agencies and specialists—generally results from two dangerous behaviors: (1) The larger agency dissintermediates the specialist from the client and communication flows poorly, or (2) the specialist usurps the larger agency's account function and threatens the agency's position. Savvy clients can sense this is happening when one agency individual (whether a sister-agency employee or consultant) bemoans another. Clients have low tolerance for refereeing between competing individuals from what is presumed to be a single team. That said, an experienced client can mitigate this risk by defining roles and identifying accountability at various stages. For instance, as a client, I expect to speak directly to the creative team when developing a creative brief. But I expect the account lead to manage the development of campaigns until they're ready for my input. Likewise, a marketer may wish to brainstorm with the online-video expert and have direct communication in setting a strategy and prioritizing tactics. The marketer then might expect the account lead to oversee execution but the specialist to return at select phases (like approvals or review of metrics).

6. Make a Black-and-White List. In emerging forms of advertising, there will be winners and losers among specialty firms. For example, a niche firm (word-of-mouth expert, video production firm, video distribution specialist) may lack skill beyond its core competency. In other cases, a good firm may execute poorly even in its sweet spot because of an incompetent individual. An agency needs to keep tabs on vendors and programs that succeed and fail, and determine if the cause was: (1) poor strategy or direction, (2) a weak specialty firm, (3) ill-defined roles or communication, or (4) a simple personality clash.

7. Separating the People. An excellent example is the way agencies have teamed with YouTube stars. That means tracking both the performance of the medium (YouTube) *and* the partner (an online-video specialist) who managed the assignment. A success is probably indicative that both are solid. But a failure could mean one or the other is falling short, and knowing the right answer will be important in determining if another attempt should be made.

8. Timing Is Everything. On one hand, few want to be the first to pilot something, as it's hard to predict outcomes, much less scope the time it will take to see results. When an agency has trouble and a simple project gets bloated, it either needs to reevaluate how it did it or determine that it's a cost-prohibitive tactic because of the manpower it consumes. On the other hand, by the time it's 100 percent clear that a social-media tactic does, in fact, work, it will most likely be an antiquated one. There's an African proverb that sums this up nicely: "If you wait for the whole beast to appear before throwing the spear, you're already too late."

At a 2010 advertising conference (Ad-Tech), I led a session called "Internet's Funniest People." Via Disney's "Take180" group, we tapped a Barack Obama impersonator (known as Alphacat on YouTube) to jokingly impose government standards on advertisers. The gag advertisers seemed to find most humorous was Obama's insistence that all advertisers be mandated to use "user-generated content" in lieu of professionally produced productions. Most agencies understandably resent the idea of ceding creative tasks to amateur producers or directors. While there is no shortage of talented lower-cost creators (who can be accessed through such specialists as Poptent.org or Hitviews), most agencies prefer to produce their own content.

Still, the fragmentation of media requires more video creative that fits certain microsegments, and experienced Web-video creators can help reduce costs and increase views. The most progressive digital agencies have begun to enlist semipro creators with less overhead, and tap webstars who already have an audience and know what works in this evolving medium.

Cautionary Case Study: The Snack Food Online Video Promo You'll Never See

Members of the marketing team of a major consumer-packaged-goods product once discovered my videos through an online-video contest, and decided they wanted to commission a yearlong series of custom videos to help launch a significant line extension. A YouTube sales representative arranged a meeting with me and the brand team, and we developed a comprehensive plan that involved my custom content and a large advertising spend on YouTube. The project was so significant, it was part of my impetus to quit my day job and focus entirely on online video.

The client requested its digital agency to lead the project, and the agency's first decision was to eliminate a robust YouTube advertising spend and to commission three pilot videos. I worked with the digital agency's creative lead to ensure my video balanced the needs of the brand and the audience. We developed a concept for the first video, and I promptly shot some candid-camera-style videos with my young son. The videos showed him conducting taste tests between the new snack food and odd foods like asparagus and parsnips. Alas, the brand team (or its attorneys) felt the vegetable comparisons would upset health advocates, and we reshot the video to include a range of other food items. I shot at least 12 different versions of the video, and attorneys eventually terminated the project. The client's legal team ultimately saw the video promotion not as product placement, but as an advertising asset they needed to own like a television commercial. They asked the interactive agency to transfer perpetual rights of the video and indemnify them from any issues such as talent rights and copyrights. The digital agency lost money on the project, and I was never paid.

This experience begged some significant questions about a branded approach to online video:

- What is the role of the distribution site (YouTube) versus the digital agency?

- What should YouTube do if marketers circumvent advertising spending and pay creators directly?

- Would custom videos be viewed as product placement or a controlled advertisement?

- Who "owns" the video? The client or the creator?

Contrast this convoluted experience with my first sponsored video in 2007. I was contacted directly by a Mentos product director, and he explained his goals. I sent him a creative brief and some concepts, and he approved them in a short phone call. I shot the video without talent release forms, and sent him the footage. We went through two edits, and the video was posted weeks later with a simple "thanks to Mentos for supporting this video" disclaimer.

I was thrilled to receive what I'd now consider a trivial payment. He later asked if he could use the video in paid advertising on Break.com and Google Video, and I was so excited I didn't even consider charging him for rights. I reedited the video for a 30-second format and even created custom display ads for his use. He ended up hiring me for a series of additional videos that were seen in excess of a million times. Alas, lawyers and intermediaries have their place, but can sabotage innovation.

The Battle of the Bands

Social media and online video are highly contentious topics in corporations. Before marketers can engage, they face challenges internally and externally. Each department feels these mediums are their jurisdiction, and tactics are debated by cross-functional teams that include marketing, public relations, technology, legal, and additional departments that otherwise may not frequently communicate with one another.

The agencies are also grappling over who takes the lead on these programs. Each agency has account leads who know their clients intimately, and functional experts who know various mediums inside and out (print, television, online). A brand's success in online video requires understanding of the brand's strategy and the unique dynamics of the medium. Few agencies have employees capable of both. I will simplify the perspective of various players, and this varies depending on the individual companies and account leaders.

- The *agency of record* (AOR) drives a brand's strategic and creative approach, and regards its role as "alpha male" among the agency dog pack. If a brand is deploying in social media or online video, the AOR wants the approach, messaging, and creative to be consistent and integrated with other forms of advertising.

- The interactive agency is more familiar with the Internet, and resents the AOR's control. For a decade, it has struggled to adapt the brand's approach to the digital medium, holding to the belief that Facebook and YouTube are its domain.

- The public relations firm is focused less on pushing a controlled message, and more on the influence of media and issue management. Most PR firms increasingly recognize that small-time bloggers can shape the perspectives of journalists. However, with a few exceptions, the PR firm lacks Internet-savvy account teams and, at best, has a *social-media guru* who is stretched across various clients.

- The media agency is charged with consolidating the purchase of online and offline media and focusing on paid placement, which is an important aspect to an online-video strategy but hardly comprehensive.

Clients tend to vacillate between two approaches to agency management, and they swing like a pendulum between the two extremes. In some instances, clients prefer a "best of breed" approach with selective agencies that are experts at particular domains. This brings functional strength, but often at the expense of an integrated approach. Furthermore, it can be more expensive and complicated, as agencies quarrel and blame one another when things don't pan out as planned. Eventually, a marketing executive then decides on a single agency to manage the brand's various functions and mediums via a major holding company (often autonomous experts that are centrally owned but independently operated). Holding companies profess to utilize a coordinated approach, and sometimes create a separate division focused on a client or industry. Experienced clients or agency veterans will confess that this is easier to claim than to actualize. The individual experts continue to battle, sometimes concealing this from clients.

How does this impact a marketer's approach to online video? Generally, the account team is unfamiliar with the nuances of the medium, but afraid to allow their functional experts to have direct contact with the client. If the agency holding company has an online-video expert, he or she may inadvertently contradict the agency's strategy, or reveal limited understanding of the client. The account leader wants to protect the client from some of the complicated details of online video, and the medium expert wants to ensure that the brand optimizes its tactical approach. It is difficult to find someone who is bilingual, and can speak the language of a brand and translate that to an evolving online-video landscape.

Letting Go Can Be Hard to Do

It was difficult being among the first digital agencies to introduce the Internet to corporations that sought control. Traditional marketers initially had a love-hate relationship with the Internet: They weren't sure they wanted their brands participating in the Wild West of the Web, and they wanted to control the experience in a medium that is not completely controllable. While at Johnson & Johnson (J&J), I used to devour statistics about online growth and help brands realize that their target was indeed on the Web. Next, I would urge them to develop their own controlled presence, but recognize that a web site is not a Web strategy. There were other equally important tactics to help them remain relevant to their audience, and this required online advertising, paid search, and engagement with other web sites and blogs.

As the Internet progressed, Wikipedia was a reminder that the Internet does not allow a brand to control its image in the way broadcast and print advertising permits. This felt academic until a Wikipedia page emerged for my own "Nalts" brand, and I realized that I couldn't control *my* image.

One of my favorite case studies of online video involves Coke and Mentos. Peaking in 2006, videos were widely spread that showed the explosive effects of inserting a few Mentos candies into a bottle of diet Coke or Pepsi. This prompted Mentos to harness the phenomenon by sponsoring video creators. Coke, by contrast, initially distanced itself from the fad because it did not perceive the game to be consistent with Coke's image. In time, my former J&J colleague, Michael Donnelly, convinced Coke to tap into the excitement. Donnelly sponsored two performers, EepyBird (see Figure 7.1), who had already created videos featuring elaborate Coke and Mentos fountains

Figure 7.1 The Coke-Mentos fountain phenomenon. EepyBird brought attention to Coke and Mentos via visual cinema that went viral.

(and had earned more than $50,000 on revenue-sharing Revver.com). Soon Eepybird was performing at events with support provided by Coke.

Public Relations versus Marketing

Two of my most frustrating moments at Johnson & Johnson concerned online video and social media (although we were then calling it *blogging*). I worked in the migraine category and was tremendously frustrated that searches for "migraine" on Google Video, YouTube, and other sites yielded little more than a short film called "migraine." For months, I struggled to convince our attorneys, regulators, and public relations groups to permit the brand to upload some educational content that I knew would get top billing. This was, to me, low-hanging fruit, but it begged questions about who would manage this content, how it would remain updated, and what policies we would follow.

Another career-defining moment came when I observed a prominent blogger who chronicled her headaches daily. The patient suffered from migraines, and had the same level of influence on migraine patients as did journalists or published physicians. I read her posts reprimanding the advertising of our competitors, and knew what would work. As a fellow blogger, I held companies in high esteem if they were interacting with me on a personal level. It is hard to trash a company that has reached out to you with a kind note. So I wrote the blogger and told her I would value her input on both our branded web site and educational resources. It was a calculated risk because from reading her posts, I felt that she would likely feel less insulted by our campaigns. Indeed, she was kind, and wrote me a long and entirely positive e-mail about what she liked about our web sites and how we identified with her as a patient.

Then the blogger did something I had not entirely expected, but was thrilled about. She posted my questions (without identifying me personally) and her positive answers. Before I discovered this on my own, I received an urgent call from our public relations director. The director understood my innocuous intent, but saw my e-mail as circumventing her team and as an act of recklessness since we had not yet developed proper guidelines. The director's boss, who was until that moment an enthusiastic supporter of me, read me the riot act. He characterized my outreach as treason and potentially out of compliance with federal laws. I saw my e-mail as informal research, but he saw it as in conflict with Federal Drug Administration guidelines, and ultimately, grounds for termination.

Meanwhile, I literally received a bear hug from our vice president of marketing, and the president of the operating company was thrilled. Since they were higher on the corporate food chain, I received immunity. And my self-imposed penance for my PR sins was a first draft of a social-media policy, which did not get ratified and communicated until three years later.

Online-Video Creator as Producer or Distributor?

Popular online-video creators have two things to offer brands, and few agencies recognize both. First, they have a rare ability to determine what approach will resonate with their audiences. Second, they have an audience.

Agencies sometimes approach partnerships by treating the video creator as a subcontractor, because this is how they manage freelance directors and producers. Eventually, some realize that the polished video production deployed for paid advertisements is inappropriate and unnecessary for online video. Yet few agencies want to see their client videos shot by a $500 video camera and edited by an amateur.

The best illustration of this involved a wildly popular YouTube singer who was hired in 2007 by a leading soft-drink manufacturer to promote a new beverage. The agency paid the creator to do a parody of his most-viewed video, which is now approaching 50 million views. It hired a production company to give the video a bolder look than the singer's previous hits. We could argue about whether that was worthwhile, but the video was, in my opinion, well done. It was overproduced, but irreverent and funny. The singer maintained some creative control, and the brand took a backseat to entertainment. However, the agency made one tremendous mistake that demonstrates a deep misunderstanding of the medium. It posted the video on its own channel, and it was not widely seen. The singer, as a gesture rather than out of contractual obligation, then posted the same video on his own channel, and it was eventually seen nearly 10 million times.

The agency had contracted the singer for a video production, and failed to realize the primary benefit of his involvement: an embedded audience.

"Branded Entertainment," the Oxymoron?

Branded entertainment is an elusive ecosystem of its own, riddled with high-profile failures, including the short-lived online-video studios and BudTV. Smart studios and agencies have shifted away from creating content with hopes of finding an advertiser. Now, brands can identify which content their target audience already watches, and work more

Figure 7.2 A parody of Generi-Tech shows when well-intended brand control can suffocate the entertainment value of the medium.

creatively with them as a result. It's a catch-22, of course. The producers are reluctant to bankroll content and search out an audience without advertiser commitment. However, advertisers ought not to be using ad dollars to promote a show or they'll likely overcommercialize it.

I am a big fan of a clever parody video about branded entertainment showing the CollegeHumor guys struggling with a fictional company, "Generi-Tech," which wants to brand the heck out of their video (see Figure 7.2).[1] Of course, the client sets the stage by saying it doesn't want to interfere with the creator's voice.

In my experience, the marketer interferes with creatives in subtler but equally amusing ways. The biggest challenge for branded entertainment is meeting the marketing or legal requirements without muting the humor.

CHAPTER 8

Learning from Online-Video "Stars"

In this chapter, you will learn:

- About the online video stars, or *webstars*, who have garnered significant and loyal followings. You have not heard of most of them, but they have daily audiences larger than many television shows.

- How online video is similar to the advent of radio, television, and film in creating new stars who are uniquely suited to the medium.

- The various skills that make a video star successful, and how networks and marketers can learn from them and their enormous, recurring audience.

The Webstar Is Born

In covering online video over several years, I have made some accurate predictions. But I remain wrong about one. As I mentioned in Chapter 1, I have previously predicted this age of the amateur to be fleeting, and expected video stars to soon be surpassed by higher-quality production.

In reality, however, today's most-subscribed YouTube Partners are not networks, web series, or musicians. They are individual amateurs and semiprofessional content creators. Their audience views them as a virtual friend—a star who talks back to them, unlike those on television and film.

Many marketers are focused on creating a viral video, but they are missing the reach and influence of a sustainable audience via online video. Search out the most-viewed online-video personalities (TubeMogul.com/marketplace), and you will find an emerging breed of stars with recurring and enormous audiences online. Since these individuals are generally one-man bands, they have low costs and are eager for even modest sponsorships. It has been exciting to help major brands tap into their influence with incredible results. It is also rewarding to help a fellow video creator make money doing what he or she loves.

Fox Broadcasting campaign tapped these webstars to promote a line of new television shows (*Lie to Me*, *Fringe*, *Glee*) to nearly 10 million individuals via online video. I helped create, develop, and measure the campaign as a consultant for Hitviews (see Figure 8.1). Hitviews is a New York City company that matches brands with Internet video's most-watched stars. The company tapped into a significant audience via dozens of webstars and gave Fox a return on investment that rivals almost any form of marketing.

Walter Sabo, one of the youngest VPs of radio and television, founded Hitviews in 2007. Sabo secured investments from some of the most-recognized players of traditional media (including Bob Weinstein, cofounder of Miramax, and The Weinstein Brothers) and recruited Caitlin Hill

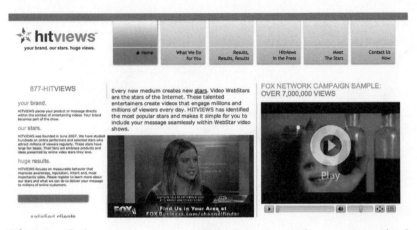

Figure 8.1 Hitviews matches brands with most-watched webstars.

(TheHill88) from Australia. Hill recruited dozens of leading video creators to participate in campaigns, and now provides marketers with demographics on each one (see Figure 8.2). Sabo calls us stars, but I hesitate to use that term to refer to online-video creators. We are not invited to red-carpet events or covered often on *Entertainment Tonight*. So *webstars* just seems like a better fit.

Sabo's vision of a webstar has proven to be quite accurate. As Sabo tells it: "Every new medium creates new stars." Sabo should know, as he was instrumental in discovering Dr. Ruth, and received investments from his friend Bruce Morrow (Morrow, known as "Cousin Brucie," who introduced the Beatles on their August 23, 1966, concert in Shea Stadium).

Indeed, history has shown that each media evolution (from radio, film, and television to Web video) creates new stars. Charlie Chaplin pioneered film. Video killed the radio star. MTV Video Jockey Adam Curry pioneered podcasting. And who was Felix the Cat before television? Nathan Lane can sell out Broadway, but has had several failed sitcoms.

Figure 8.2 Hitviews, founded by radio and television executives and a YouTube star (Caitlin Hill) helps companies tap webstars to reach large audiences.

While some stars transcend film and television, online video has created a new batch of stars. I am always amazed when I present my findings to marketers and ask them who has heard of "Fred," the 16-year-old alter ego of a Nebraska teenager named Lucas Cruikshank. Few hands are raised, despite Fred's more than half billion views online. By contrast, Oprah's presence in online video is trivial.

What Does a Webstar Do for a Living?

As I began this book, I could count on one hand my friends who make their full-time living from their online-video presence. Now, dozens of amateurs have quit their day jobs and are living comfortably from YouTube advertising sharing and revenue from sponsored videos.

I have long been skeptical of the sustainability of this model, but it continues. First-time documentary maker

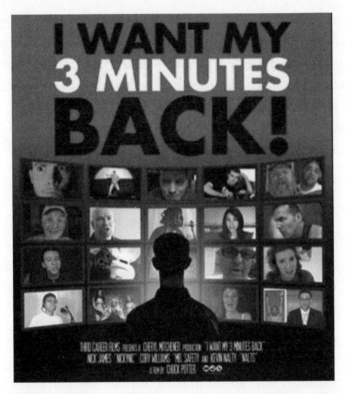

Figure 8.3 A documentary titled "I Want My Three Minutes Back" chronicles the trials and tribulations of well-known webstars through several years.

Chuck Potter captured the journey of several webstars (including myself) over the course of several years. The film "I Want My Three Minutes Back" takes the viewer deep into the lives of these individuals in their struggles to reach and maintain their so-called fame. (See Figure 8.3.)

The conventional myth about these webstars is that they're using the medium to ascend to careers in television and film. In fact, that has not proven to work. Lisa Donovan, who is known online as "LisaNova," did a brief stint on *MADtv*. Fred Lucas (Fred) held a cameo on Nickelodeon's *iCarly*.[1] An HBO Labs series gave a dozen of us a chance to prove our acting chops in a series called *Hooking Up* (naturally, I played a jaded college professor while my friends played students). But in reality, most webstars are satisfied with the income and creative freedom they have, and many can't act.

Acting, of course, is just one talent that makes a webstar. There are dozens more:

- One-Man Bands: While some webstars now have agents and staff, most are self-sufficient. They produce, write, act, edit, distribute, and promote their own content. Sometimes they're a duo (Rhett & Link, Smosh, Barats & Bereta) and sometimes they form groups ("TheStation" is a collection of popular YouTube webstars), but usually it's one individual.

- Persistence: The most common attribute among webstars is persistence. It is easier to create a one-time viral hit than sustain an audience over several years. Most webstars are like fads, and they tend to peak and fade in a predictable 6- to 18-month period. Others continue to reinvent, and somehow manage to stay true to themselves while experimenting with new content to avoid audience fatigue.

- Thick Skin: A webstar is more accessible to direct audience feedback, and manages to enjoy the praise while becoming immune to the 2 to 5 percent of abusive comments from anonymous viewers.

- Self-Driven: Most webstars are drawn to the medium by more than fame and fortune, and needless to say, they are self-motivated. It is not easy to work independently and develop new ideas, follow internal creative drives, and satisfy audiences.

- Marketers: There are shy webstars and outgoing ones, but most are successful self-promoters. I'd call many of them *accidental marketers*. They find an unmet niche and cater to it. They promote their content instinctively, and adapt to the changing trends. They detect what content is succeeding and adapt accordingly. A typical video may take one to six hours, but most webstars spend hours each day watching other creators, answering e-mails, and studying what works and what doesn't work.

Case Study: Discovery Is a Shark

After music and television networks, the Discovery network is one of the most popular YouTube Partners based on professional content. This is not entirely due to the channel's distinct advantage of having shark footage (Figure 8.4).

Discovery has mimicked the best practices of amateur creators, while other networks appear to have channels managed by a summer intern with messy hair. Oprah, whose YouTube presence languishes despite some promotion at launch, could learn much from Discovery. Oprah's videos average a mere 3,000 to 5,000 views per video.

Here are some examples of how Discovery's YouTube presence resembles that of a webstar:

- Brilliant move: Post microclips like a surprise shark attack. A video annotation notes, "SURPRISE SHARK ATTACK" on another Discovery clip. How can you not click that?

- We soon realize that the individual identifying himself as a combat diver, technical diver, and former member

Figure 8.4   Unlike many professional shows, YouTube's Discovery Channel employs proven tactics that are otherwise used exclusively by YouTube amateurs.

of the Marine Corps special ops unit known as Force Recon is not going to get chewed by a shark. Another annotation appears: "Watch this decoy leap—CLICK HERE." See what's happening? Discovery is hooking my attention like a fisherman catching a great white shark.

- Discovery's branded options include an amateur-like banner that begs viewers to subscribe.

- Discovery was one of the first content providers to purchase yellow ads that promote content in related videos.

- Now, what if I decide to subscribe? I am invited to subscribe to additional Discovery Channel networks. They must know that if they jammed all of this into one channel, I'd unsubscribe.

• What more could Discovery do? Put a human face toward the YouTube community, and vlog occasionally. And of course, respond to comments.

As I have drafted this book, Discovery has gone from 100,000 to more than 200,000 subscribers. The fact that it has surpassed my subscriber number is remarkable because I'm a combat Tuber, technical Tuber, and former member of the Viral Video special ops unit known as Force Promotion.

CHAPTER 9
Marketing via Webstars

In this chapter, you will learn:

- How brands have partnered with webstars to create entertaining promotion that is more credible and difficult to ignore than traditional online advertising.

- The benefits and challenges of identifying a webstar who fits a brand, and how to manage the process to balance the audience and marketing needs.

- Some examples of highly visible campaigns that tap webstars to augment advertising campaigns.

Earlier we identified three layers of brand content, and webstars are a cost-efficient way to reach large audiences. Brands are increasingly augmenting traditional display advertisements with investments in sponsored content and branded entertainment via online-video stars with an existing audience.

A webstar is usually an individual who has an authentic and regular connection with a growing audience, and has as many as 100,000 to 1 million subscribers. These subscribers are fans who request an alert when new videos are posted.

For instance, I'm one of the "most-viewed comedians" on YouTube with 175,000 subscribers and more than 150 million views to date. I have no agent, no staff, no production team, and no writers. But my videos are seen hundreds of thousands of times each day. We webstars aren't stalked by paparazzi or chased for autographs, but we have an intimate relationship with our loyal audiences. Our viewers interact with us, make video replies to our videos, and tell others about us. The webstar is not necessarily a polished performer, but his interactive relationship with the audience makes him highly influential to a dedicated mass of people.

Most brands and agencies do not yet realize they can now scale campaigns via these webstars by asking them to carry their branded messages in transparent and authentic ways, which are perceived by audiences as more inviting than interruption advertising. In fact, the webstar-sponsored videos, videos that are sponsored by whoever the webstar is marketing for, are often as entertaining as their regular videos.

To discover some webstars, see TubeMogul.com/marketplace (Figure 9.1), where some of the leading amateurs (and some professionals) are listed by total views.

When I have posted sponsored videos, they are seen as many as a million times because of my base audience and because I ensure they're entertaining. Webstars, videos are rated highly (which gives them increased views), and receive hundreds and thousands of positive comments. The same video posted on an unknown YouTube account would likely get no views, unless supported with pay-per-view or additional ad dollars driving viewers to the video. The loyal, embedded audience is the difference.

Unlike consumer-generated media, sponsored videos are not posted until approved by the client.

Figure 9.1 TubeMogul tracks leading video producers across more than a dozen web sites, giving brands another route to identify opportunities for sponsorship or product placement.

When these videos are seen by hundreds of thousands of fans, they create impact that rivals many online-media advertising spends—especially display ads and often paid search. While brands are paying as much as $30,000 for a single video, the cost per view or cost per engagement can vary dramatically. Some webstars get millions of views, and others get thousands. Hitviews, however, guarantees views because it works with webstars who have consistent and loyal audiences, and engages dozens of them to achieve campaign goals for our clients.

Until recently, a brand wanting to promote via a webstar would need to find the right star (which can be tricky), establish a contract with that person, then hope the star would meet the brand's objectives while still ensuring the video entertained and influenced large audiences in the brand's target market. As a career marketer, I know how fickle webstars can be in the eyes of business executives. Some refuse to make sponsored videos, others will miss deadlines, and still others have tantrums when a brand provides required revisions.

Challenges

Marketers and their agencies tend to have a difficult time communicating with webstars. The marketer in me is decisive, impatient, and obsessed with targeting customers and driving sales. The creator in me is sensitive, procrastinating, egoistic, and temperamental.

My sister, a news producer, lived in New York City and California, and refers to the rest of the country as "fly-by states." Indeed, the impatient Madison Avenue and expressive Hollywood are on two different coasts of the United States, and her perspective has perhaps arisen out of necessity.

As a marketer, I have discovered that it is rarely scalable for brands or agencies to work individually with webstars. As marketers awaken to the influence and reach of online-video stars, we'll see more sponsored videos. That is one of the reasons why, despite doing a lot of direct work for brands, I have consulted with Hitviews. Brokering between brands and webstars is difficult to do well when it's not a primary focus of a company, and Hitviews was founded to solve this need. YouTube occasionally matches brands with creators, but continues to avoid becoming a competitor of studios and agencies. At a recent conference, I spoke with a YouTube leader who corrected me when I referred to YouTube as a network. YouTube, she reminded me, is a platform.

The challenge of being the translator between a creative individual and a client is not new to agencies, but it carries new dimension when dealing with webstars. Some agencies and brands have treated webstars like outsourced producers, and that's almost guaranteed to fail. The right intermediary can translate the brand objectives into language that captivates the creators and keeps them focused. More important, someone has to know whose side to take when there's a conflict. If the "star" is being stubborn about a minor client change, then he or she needs to be told so diplomatically. In other cases, the client may have an unrealistic sense of how promotional the videos should be. I have worked on dozens of these campaigns, and have seen this handled both exquisitely and disastrously.

There are so many factors critical to making this work—finding the right webstars (some are distinctively better at this than others), handling them appropriately, and brokering revisions. This is a specialty skill set that will grow in criticality as the medium matures.

Comparing "Star Endorsement" to a Typical Advertisement

A webstar's "branded storytelling" or "star endorsement" video should not be seen as an alternative to paid advertising, but as a way to create deeper impressions than can occur in most modes of online marketing. Yet many media buyers have been assessing these promotional videos using metrics with which they're familiar—cost per impression, cost per click, and engagement rates.

Hitviews, which has conducted campaigns for such brands as Fox, MTV, Microsoft, and *Reader's Digest*, analyzed its recent campaigns according to these metrics and found that its vehicle beat typical online spending, even if measured in the most conservative way possible: cost-per-view or cost-per-minute engagement.

Costs per View: Online Video Compared to Other Mediums

If a popular online-video or Web-video series contains a promotion integrated as part of entertaining or informative videos, the sponsor has three advantages:

1. The message is more likely to be seen.

2. The ROI is higher because fixed and variable costs are low (relative to similar mediums) and engagement rates are high (as measured by view duration and/or measurable tasks like rating or clicking a link).

3. Finally, the audience trusts the webstar, and the promotion is perceived as an implied endorsement. In television terms, this is akin to Jimmy Kimmel promoting a product within the show, or an *American Idol* judge drinking a Coke during the program. Furthermore, the promotion is perpetually and inextricably tied to the content, so it's a lasting residual for the brand and travels with the video around the Internet, unlike other paid ad media, because it's not an ad; it's content.

The promotional or sponsored videos typically outperform traditional online and offline advertising spending even on the most conservative dimensions. Here are some data from Hitviews campaigns with major brands:

- Some Hitviews campaigns provided sponsors with a cost per view of less than 10 cents per view (assuming a conservative one-and-a-half-minute view of an average video length of three minutes, which is a stronger cost-per-engagement statistic than any other medium).

- Where one advertiser was seeking to drive visits to a micro site, the collective webstar videos drove approximately 6 to 12 percent of viewers. That created an average cost per visit of approximately 50 cents, which rivals paid search (and that does not include the video's impact beyond driving traffic).

- Although a cost-per-1,000 (CPM) banner buy may drive impressions for significantly less, eye-tracker studies have shown that most impressions aren't seen. Although well-targeted and well-placed banners (above the fold) can drive awareness with frequency, the cost per click is exponentially higher.

- The engagement rates for banners are often cost prohibitive. Moderate banner clickthrough rates (0.01 to 5 percent, or even using the estimate of Pointroll, a rich-media advertising technology company, of 3 to 5 percent engagement for rich media ads) produce cost per engagement of $0.50 to $7.00 (assuming CPM prices of $7.00 to $30.00).

- CPM is an artificial measure of impressions, and many are never seen. As I mentioned earlier, "an impression isn't an impression unless it makes one." Fox Broadcasting had one of its most successful television debuts with a show called *Lie to Me*, and Hitviews' webstars created dozens of views seen millions of times (see Figure 9.2). The videos sparked an online game where webstars created videos confessing two truths and a lie about themselves, and viewers had to guess which fact was

Figure 9.2 Even television networks recognize the value of webstars. Fox reached millions of viewers to launch *Lie to Me* and *Fringe*, and tapped Hitviews to promote to active online-video audiences.

> a lie. The game became so popular that other leading webstars participated even without compensation.

- Video engagement rates have been much higher than the 0.01 to 5 percent of banner ads, with video clickthrough rates ranging from 2 to 11 percent (as measured by comments, video replies, and ratings). More important, the video viewer is engaged in the content and more likely to internalize the message, leave a comment, or make a response video.

Ultimate Model to Measure Impact

- Currently, the ROI appears more favorable for webstars (versus other forms of online advertising) because the cost per engaged minute is significantly better than for any other medium. A higher CPM for webstars gives the brand one to three minutes of engaged viewer attention. This cannot be compared easily to banner buys that get low visibility and poor interaction rates.

- Ultimately, third-party research by companies (Dynamic Logic, Insight Express, or comScore) needs to compare the test/control impact (awareness, intent, purchase) of ads surrounding videos against in-show sponsored messages via webstars.

- The ultimate measure of impact will be test/control or pre/post research on awareness, intent, and purchase. Webstars, especially when coupled with adjacent or overlay banner ads, will provide brands with the most effective spend for gaining reach and engagement.

Why Big Brands Do and Don't Tap Webstars

As the recession hit marketers, there has been little sign of cooling in the sponsored video segment. Online-video viewing continues to grow, and advertising dollars are shifting to sites like YouTube. Increasingly, leading brands are going beyond traditional display advertising to tap webstars. Interestingly, the analyst estimates (of 40 to 60 percent growth) often neglect to capture these programs.

Webstars offer advertisers a higher-impact model to reach an engaged audience—one who eagerly awaits their next video. The audience trusts the star, and engages via comments and video responses. Since webstars are often twentysomethings with a low cost of living, they are open to sponsorships and product placements. Sponsored videos can produce far more monthly income than YouTube advertising sharing.

Figure 9.3　Carl's Jr. promoted its new burger via top web-stars, and it gave them the creative freedom to suit their style and audience.

When I was working as a product director, I found a video *about* my brand exponentially more valuable than ads alone. As a traditional-media analog, consider the difference between a 30-second ad on *American Idol* and Coke cups appearing on the actual *Idol* judges' table. The latter is an implied endorsement by the judges (and you may hate two of them, but probably not all four).

Many leading brands—TiVo, GE, Carl's Jr., Fox, and others—are using webstars, while other brands are focusing exclusively on interruption advertising. Carl's Jr. sponsored dozens of webstars in a campaign to promote a new burger, and the videos were seen millions of times (see Figure 9.3). Given the efficiency of this program, it would seem intuitive that most major advertisers would be initiating similar programs. Why aren't they?

1. Most brands and even their agencies cannot establish relationships with webstars on their own. They don't know the webstars or their videos well enough to know if they fit the brand's personality, much less if the webstar is reliable.

2. The bigger stars are primarily focused on their audiences, and not branding or even business. That means agencies may be surprised that the video creators aren't kowtowing to them like subcontractors.

3. Agencies and brands are just beginning to understand that sponsored videos are becoming both common and appropriate in social media (as long as the sponsor is disclosed and the content is entertaining). Few know this medium offers the control their brands need (final review of content's tone and message). The webstar won't read from a script, of course, but the brand sponsor typically approves the concept and the final video.

4. The creative challenge is to entertain first and promote second. That requires sponsors to give the stars some creative freedom and trust their instincts. Almost all three of my Fox videos were cleared without edits, but one food manufacturer ultimately required such control of the content that after 12 revisions, its attorneys pulled the assignment from the agency that hired me.

5. Online-video stars sometimes have agents, but often are one-man bands. That means some are professional, and others are immature in their business dealings. What made them popular with viewers, such as being edgy and autonomous, can undermine them when

it's time to face such things as deadlines and review processes.

6. Finding stars takes significant knowledge of the online-video community. Some are easy to work with, and others are a nightmare. Some get top views, but have images and videos that are not right for certain brands. Some are inexpensive, and others demand top dollars.

I have seen few of these campaigns run effectively without an intermediary—whether it's Hitviews, YouTube, an agency, or a Web studio. In fact, it's nearly impossible for brands and agencies to tap these video creators without an intermediary. An exception was when a product director of Mentos became my first client, and was surprisingly hands-off with the creative but focused when it came to his audience and message.

As a video creator, I've dealt with agencies that think of webstars as subcontractors and want an advertisement instead of an entertaining video that promotes a brand by default. For this model to scale, it needs companies that can broker the relationship so the three key constituents (brand, creator, and audience) can get what they need:

1. First, audiences must like the videos. Failing that, nothing else matters.

2. Second, the "star" must feel comfortable with the brand, and feel compensated appropriately. The videos take time, but more important, an excess of them will harm their relationship with the audience. I have continually increased my price for sponsored videos because frequency of sponsored videos can create audience fatigue.

3. Finally, the advertiser (a brand team or its steward) must feel like its money is well spent, and the sponsored video must be regarded as worth more than a pre-roll, overlay, or banner. Few agencies understand how to compare a view of a sponsored video with a banner ad, and I know that will change. If agencies see this model as nothing more than a media buy, it will be undervalued and marginalized.

CHAPTER 10
Paid Video Advertising

In this chapter, you will learn:

- Why most video start-ups have failed.

- How to make money via online video if you're willing to invest time.

- What video content will engage your audience instead of making them feel "pitched."

- About another attempt at the Web-studio model that may work—or not.

Most marketers, especially those accustomed to buying television advertising, will marginalize their investments in online video to paid advertising. Without a doubt, the medium depends on advertising support since few have yet proven that *subscription* or *pay-per-episode* models can work. The paid play related to video has gone through several Darwinian evolutions:

1. **Penny Ads.** Initially, online-video sites had difficulty convincing advertisers to place ads adjacent to consumer-generated video. Most of the early advertising revenue was generated by discounted cost-per-impression ads that were literally pennies

per thousand impressions. This hardly offset the infrastructure costs, but minimal revenue and copyright problems did not stop Google from seeing long-term value in owning the largest video-sharing property.

2. **Home-Page Featured Videos.** YouTube was only able to attract advertisers for home-page placements (Quicken annually promoted its software via a promotional video on YouTube's home page). Soon, savvy viewers realized what YouTube calls a "video companion ad" or an "expandable autoplay video ad" (see Figure 10.1) was not entertainment, and they avoided it. I met a Quicken marketing executive at an Interactive media conference in Florida years ago, and

Figure 10.1   YouTube viewers began to recognize the home-page player as an advertisement and avoid it. So YouTube began to rotate "paid placement" videos with unsponsored content in such areas as "Spotlighted" or "Related" videos.

asked him if he had seen views decline in his third year of the campaign. He was surprised I knew of this, and I explained that viewers had been trained to avoid the home-page player. He was undaunted, however, because YouTube helped him reach his target by promoting the video through other areas of the site.

3. **Quiet "Pay to Play" Campaigns.** Few video-sharing sites will admit that they have featured videos for advertisers, often charging 5 to 10 cents for every view. For instance, the featured videos on YouTube (see Figure 10.2) are a combination of popular videos and those supported with advertising dollars. I once needed to reach a target for a viral video series I inherited, which was getting paltry organic views. I approached a third-tier video-sharing site with $10,000 in advertising, and my videos reached 1 million views within days. This model still exists, and web sites use terms like *spotlighted* or *promoted* videos, and then mix paid videos with popular ones to entice viewers.

4. **Partner Program.** YouTube was finally able to attract major advertisers by developing the Partner Program, which vets the quality, tone, and copyrights

Featured Videos

Star Wars Film Set
Goes WRONG! '...
3 weeks ago
214,681 views
Zipster08

Weekend Project:
Compressed Air ...
2 weeks ago
192,602 views
Mugglesam

Into The Universe
With Stephen H...
3 weeks ago
80,974 views
Nutcheese

Friday Dr Pepper
Ultimate Highli...
2 weeks ago
46,751 views
Lemonette

Figure 10.2 Featured videos on YouTube mix popular content with videos that command higher advertising revenue.

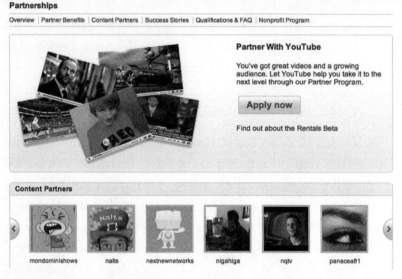

Figure 10.3 YouTube's Partner Program gives professionals and amateurs the ability to share a percentage of YouTube's advertising revenue. Partners agree to copyright and "taste and tone" standards to ensure the content is "advertising safe."

of select content creators. (See Figure 10.3.) This enabled YouTube to debut its "InVideo" model (overlay ads that pop up beneath a video in the first 10 to 20 seconds). Although the offering was launched at a hefty $25 CPM (per thousand impressions), advertisers generally pay less since supply exceeds demand. I expect this dynamic to change as advertisers raise spending and conduct ROI analysis on the performance of these ads, which are far more difficult to ignore than display advertisements adjacent to videos. These ads will have moderate (low single digit) clickthrough rates, but are effective branding and awareness drivers.

5. **Home-Page Takeover.** YouTube and other sites, driven by a desire to increase profitability, began

aggressive home-page takeover advertisements in 2008 and 2009. A movie debut or new television series would dominate the vast majority of the home page with promotion, making it difficult to ignore. These programs, which also offered advertisers inventory across the site, commanded higher revenue. More important, they gave advertising agencies the ability to customize the experience for brands (generating their own creative and design revenue beyond a small percentage of the advertising spend).

6. **Brand Channels.** YouTube offers branded channels to large advertisers, and the price varies but generally starts at several hundred thousand dollars. That amount does not fund the setup cost of the branded channel (which is usually created by an agency with minor technical support from YouTube), but the advertising required to generate traffic to it via such media as InVideo ads on Partner videos. This is effective for large brands that might otherwise spend money on a micro site or campaign site and yet have paltry traffic directed to it. However, this option is somewhat cost prohibitive for small brands or start-ups. The alternative is to create a free channel, but this offers less customization (e.g., banners, links to product web sites) and requires the owner to generate traffic on his own—via paid advertising and organic approaches. As I've said before, if brands cannot justify a brand channel, I still urge them to post video content on YouTube (both to optimize search rankings and to get the videos where people are viewing videos).

7. **Integrated Campaigns.** Increasingly, advertisers are approaching YouTube as a partner, and developing custom campaigns that vary. For example, the General Electric (GE) Healthymagination campaign (which appeared extensively on television during the 2010 Olympics) tapped Howcast (an instructional-video studio) to manage a comprehensive online-video campaign to promote health. The program involved InVideo advertisements, a YouTube Howcast channel that offered health-related videos, links to GE's web site, and resources. YouTube and Howcast also tapped a number of video creators (including me) to create videos accepting health challenges from viewers. Years ago, advertisers approached me directly. Later, Hitviews secured my sponsorships via such companies as Fox Broadcasting, MTV, and Microsoft. Increasingly, YouTube has reached out to me directly to create video campaigns for Starbucks and Kodak.

The future of online advertising is best represented by companies like 7Echo, which partners with prominent content owners and advertisers to create rich-media experiences that engage and entertain audiences, and provide advertisers with custom opportunities to go beyond pre-roll ads or adjacent banners. Of course, the video-sharing site (YouTube, Yahoo! Video, Hulu) also has to have a stake, since it has the audience access and controls the functionality of the site. These rich-media experiences are otherwise destined to reside on micro sites, which would require significant advertising spend to draw sufficient traffic to offset the fixed costs of developing them.

Web Video: An Industry Out of Balance

By Jim Louderback, CEO of Revision3

In the seminal 1982 movie *Koyaanisqatsi*, life is portrayed as out of balance. These days, when I look at our online-video industry, I can't help thinking that we're just as unbalanced as that movie—particularly when it comes to driving audience and traffic.

Much of the imbalance, I think, comes from trying to retrofit the Web display model onto what is fundamentally a different medium, one that values a view much differently than a Web visit.

To illustrate, let me lay out an example of a problem I was trying to solve recently, and the obdurate obstacles I ran into. We were launching a new show in the coming weeks. And we've got a sponsor attached with the show launch, one that we've promised a certain number of video views. Now I know we're going to hit it out of the park—but I want to prepare for the worst. So I did a little research into how I might be able to drive a little bit of paid traffic to our new show.

Here's where it all falls down. Our show sponsor is paying us a very nice CPM—$80—which is far above traditional pre-rolls and overlays. We'll probably run those units as well, which could add a few dollars to the effective CPM—in a perfect world. Chances are, we'll probably end up with an effective yield per view of somewhere around a dime, which translates into a $100 CPM.

(Continued)

From what I gather, a $100 effective CPM per view is pretty amazing in today's online-video world. But what's more amazing is how much I'd have to pay to deliver a nonorganic viewer to the show.

If I had wanted to use YouTube's "Videosense" product to drive a view, I would have been required to bid the then minimum bid price of 10 cents a click (or 10 cents per view on autoplay). That means I'd just break even every time someone watches—if I'm the only bidder.

So I looked out to others who promised to deliver qualified viewers. I had an interesting exchange with one company CEO who promised to give me qualified viewers for 20 to 30 cents per view. The amazing thing, to me, was that his pricing was low compared to some of the other options I researched.

Talk about out of balance. I'd be spending a quarter to drive views that provided me less than a dime. Until we unlock the secrets of transmutation, it'll never be profitable to spend digital quarters to earn digital dimes.

But that just leads to yet another "out of balance" problem when it comes to buying video views. Because these are cost-per-click deals, we pay when the click-through happens, not when a video is completely consumed. As we've seen, even with our committed viewers, there can be significant drop-off in the first few seconds—that's why we don't count a view for our sponsors until the program has been completely delivered. And when it comes to clicking on an ad, that drop-off can be upward of 60 to 70 percent.

Not to worry, says the video industry, and legitimized by the Interactive Advertising Bureau (IAB). If someone watches for three seconds, we consider that a *video view*—even if those viewers never actually see the advertising message embedded in the video.

When I tried to explain this to my CEO friend, this was his response:

> *I see your point . . . but the pricing is what it is. If you were to buy a CPM ad unit from YouTube or anyone else the effective cost per view would be [very] high. We are buying cost-per-thousand [CPM] in bulk and arbitraging back to you on a cost-per-view basis. Right now we are mostly selling to ad agencies that are pretty accustomed to buying media.*

So this CEO, who will remain nameless, has been able to find ad agencies willing to buy video on a $200 to $300 CPM pricing for what is effectively three seconds of watching a video. I guess the greater-fool theory still works when it comes to buying video views. But from where I sit, this is no way to build a business.

In the end, I just couldn't see clear to paying quarters and making dimes. I'm comfortable with the numbers we're promising, and if we run into any issues, I guess we'll just do a make-good. But at least my customer can be confident he's getting what he paid for.

Oh, and if any of you agencies out there that are "pretty accustomed to buying media" want a better deal, drop me a line. I'll sell you a far better placement and far better results for less than a dime that'll outperform those quarters—any day of the week.

CHAPTER 11

Measuring ROI and Performance of Online Video

In this chapter, you will learn:

- That online video, while not as data-driven as paid search, is far more accountable than print and television.

- How to hold online video accountable to your business goal—whether to increase awareness or drive direct response.

I am always amused by marketers' instinctive ROI (return on investment) questions about any medium that is new to them, or that they don't understand. Typically, I translate their "What's the ROI?" inquiries to "Please convince me I'm not wasting money, and that this might help me hit my forecast." I have used various ROI models to demonstrate the impact of a campaign, and typically support it with real data (views, engagements, visits to web site), with various assumptions from a client (likelihood of a web-site visitor to purchase, lifetime value of new customer).

Online video works best for brands trying to increase awareness and to buzz efficiently, and sometimes for direct-response campaigns (like effectively driving traffic to a web site or helping sell products that cost more than $50 or $100).

There are some brands that are a bad fit for online video because: (1) their target audience is so specific that even a well-targeted campaign would be inefficient, or (2) their service or product is available only in a specific region.

Online video is not yet an efficient vehicle for targeting individuals in a specific city or state.

There are several types of clients I have turned down for a sponsored video, and diplomatically convinced them that they could not likely justify the investment. These examples will give you a sense about what product or services demand more of a guerilla-style approach:

- **A multilevel marketing campaign for a regional power company.** The company would be paying to reach individuals they couldn't serve.

- **An online retailer of clothing.** I find few people will immediately leave a video to purchase an overpriced t-shirt, and that the seller would not likely acquire sufficient sales to cover the cost.

- **A "revenue share" entrepreneur.** Many well-intentioned entrepreneurs want to pay me for the traffic I drive or as a percent of products they sell via my campaign. Some companies, like PlaceVine pay webstars based on the sales they drive (Figure 11.1).

An Impression Is Not an Impression

Although I was recently working as a product director, most of my career has been focused on digital marketing. So

Figure 11.1 PlaceVine is one of several "business exchanges" to connect advertisers and video creators for branded integration (sponsorships or product placements).

when I purchased traditional media (print, radio, display), I deferred significantly to our company's media buyer specialist and our buying agency. I pretended to understand the cost for reach and frequency, but the reality is that my eyes glazed over at promises of awareness levels and gross rating points (GRPs). They were meaningless Excel sheets with large numbers that meant little to me. I just didn't care. All I wanted to do was ensure that a dollar spent on advertising would drive sales.

At the risk of offending a media buyer, let me speak as a marketer—whose money you are trusted to spend wisely: You confuse me. You tell me I'm getting great reach and recall, but I don't care. I just want to know that my revenue increases in excess of my ad spend (hopefully three to five times as much). So when you're making a buy on the brand's behalf, please consider impact more than reach. Reach and even targeting can't move product without impact.

In the case of online video, why would anyone sponsor a show for a dime unless it had a good reason it could sell

- *Behavior:* conversion, purchase and loyalty.

- *Awareness & Intent:* Test versus control and pre and post surveys to measure brand awareness and intent.

- *Action:* Views, comments, engagement, clickthrough.

Figure 11.2   Linking video views to sales and conversions is ideal, but almost impossible. But measuring online video should go beyond "proxy" measures like "view counts," which can be misleading. Awareness and intent surveys (prepost or test versus control) are the most accurate ways for a sponsor to determine the value of campaigns.

at least 30 to 50 cents of product? Why would someone pay for a view unless that view could sell a product? There are countless studies that show that banners are not seen, so I'd need to be proven otherwise before even a 50-cent CPM buy made sense. The InVideo ads have been proven to work (Dynamic Logic) better than pre-roll or banners, but that depends on the creative and our immunity toward them. Do you honestly think this clickthrough data from last year is true today? Most important, it depends on when the ad is served, since most never finish a video (TubeMogul), and our eyes hover around the close button like Doctor Evil on the laser button.

Pre-Rolls

Numerous studies have shown that while pre-roll advertisements may not be popular, they are effective at increasing consumer awareness. When Google first tested in-stream ads in 2007, abandonment rates for pre-rolls were as high

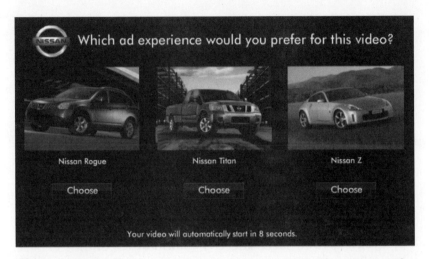

Figure 11.3   The Ad Selector gives viewers the viewer the power to choose.

as 75 percent.[1] Shorter advertising pre-rolls (15 seconds) dramatically decreased drop-off to as low as 15 percent.

Hulu introduced an "Ad Selector" (see Figure 11.3), which gives viewers the option to choose between multiple advertisements. In a recent study, an advertising firm claimed to spend 230,000 hours of research surveying 25 million consumers.[2] The Ad Selector on average delivered clickthrough rates that were 106 percent higher than pre-roll ads. Online ad-recall scores were 290 percent higher than pre-rolls—possibly due to the fact that consumers must pause and choose among several brands when using the Ad Selector.

But if the video content itself includes the brand—like Coke does with *American Idol*—it's quite hard to miss. There's also an implied endorsement because the judges (with whom we have a connection) are drinking Coke—rather than Coke boasting about the beverage. That's where the brands need to be unless our ads are as delightful as a Pixar film and we have audiences glued to their seats.

It won't matter whether analysts predict online video represents 4, 10, or 20 percent of video consumption in coming years if we can't prove it can drive sales.

Those of us championing online video have an obligation to marketers and executives to help them understand how this medium can help them.

1. **Educate.** A CPM is *not* a CPM. Simply put, a letter from a friend is going to have more impact than junk mail—even if they both arrive via the mailbox. Video ads and host-sponsored content are both delivered via video, but that's where the similarities end.

2. **Relate.** Use offline analogies. I love the Vista example Jim Lauderback used in Chapter 10. I'm not suggesting Coke bag advertising, but I have to believe there's more value in the Coke green room than the DVR-blocked ad.

3. **Substantiate.** Someone has to survey video watchers to understand—at the moment, from their perspective—what ads impact them most: an ignored banner or a trusted star or show with a good placement. If you've done it, I doubt the media buyers know.

4. **Calculate.** The Holy Grail is to show via test/control or pre/post (Dynamic Logic, comScore, Insight) that contextual and relevant video messaging is worth exponentially more than wraparound banners or existing IAB standards (see IAB report for best practices). It's intuitive, but data will make media buyers' lives easier; they know that an impression isn't an impression unless it makes an impression. Now you can get back to lunch with the media properties.

Measuring CPM versus Branded Entertainment

Unfortunately, few branded entertainment companies have measured or shared the ROI on programs. We can find many soft reports by agency case studies, but the industry needs credible third-party reports (eMarketer, Hitwise, comScore, or Forrester) for comparison.

How do you compare banner impressions to hosted endorsement in the context of the show? What's it worth when Jimmy Kimmel endorses a product on his television show? (I have heard estimates as high as $300 thousand.) As a Web example, the hosts of Film Riot (a popular show by online-video studio, Revision3) deliver their own playful Netflix ad in the middle. The ad is tucked between segments so that viewers can't easily skip it, and it is as entertaining as the rest of the show. (See Figure 11.4.)

To determine true ROI of an example like Film Riot's Netflix campaign, we would need pre/post and test/control studies, which might demonstrate that Netflix increases

Figure 11.4 Film Riot's creators make their own custom Netflix advertisements, which feel less intrusive and provide more credibility to the show's loyal audience.

recall, intent, and purchase. I would certainly expect the performance on these to far surpass that of CPM banner ads. It would be shortsighted and myopic to assess the campaign based on registered Netflix users who redeemed the discount code Film Riot provides.

A Hitviews campaign I helped conduct promoted a television network's micro site, and the webstar videos drove 6 to 12 percent of its viewers to the web site (this is rare). If the advertiser paid a nickel per view, the campaign would drive traffic to the site for 30 to 60 cents per click. Banners, by contrast, would cost $5 to $50 per visitor, and even paid search could not top those numbers or provide the reach the advertiser needed.

CHAPTER 12

Video and Search Engine Optimization

With Mark Robertson, ReelSEO

Search engines will dramatically impact your success with online video, and this will become a highly competitive area in coming years. The search engine is a broker between you and your customer for a variety of reasons:

- Your customers are increasingly using specific terms in their searches, and including the word *video* into searches more than the word *sex*. In the past five years, the term *how to* has grown steadily as a search phrase (Google Trends).[1]

- Approximately one-third of the views of a video were driven by search. It may surprise you that search engines overtook social media as a driver to videos back in early 2008.[2] Still, the race is not over.

- Google, by far the leading search engine, incorporates many forms of media in its universal search results.

Mark Robertson is the Founder of RealSEO and a leading authority on video marketing and search engine optimization.

Since it currently indexes far more text than video, you have a distinct advantage with video content.

I use the term search engine marketing (SEM) to refer broadly to two types of disciplines: (1) Paid search is when you bid on search terms, so your content appears as promotion on someone's search-results page (on Google, it's the yellow area labeled "sponsored links" that surrounds the *organic* or *natural* results; and (2) search engine optimization (SEO) refers to anything you do to make your content rank more highly in organic results. This is driven by the relevancy of your content, technical configuration of your web site and Web pages, and whether other leading web sites link to your content (which search engines count as an endorsement).

Video SEO has constantly changing "best practices" to help you make it easy for search engines to crawl and index your video, and to convince a search engine algorithm that your content is relevant to a search query.

Paid search, which can occur on traditional search engines like Google and Yahoo!, is also available on YouTube (which is now the world's second-most-used search engine). For instance, electronic retailers will bid competitively for a search phrase like "how to find the best digital camera," and pay Google if you "click" their advertisement. You, too, can bid on search terms so that your video appears when someone searches for video content.

Generally, marketers invest significant amounts on SEO optimization because it is a fixed cost, not a variable one. Furthermore, eye-tracking charts reveal that on Google, viewers' eyes tend to focus less on the ads and more on the top organic or natural results dictated by the search engine's algorithm. This is especially true for video *thumbnails* (the images representing the videos, which usually precede the titles). These thumbnails are often scanned before text is read regardless of their position on the first page of the search results. Marketers and interactive agencies work diligently on web sites, their content, and "inbound links" that will appear relevant to search engines. Media buyers also buy ads around keywords that suggest someone's looking for our product or service.

Google "Hearts" YouTube

YouTube content, not surprisingly, is indexing quite well on Google. You could accuse Google of manipulation when you see YouTube videos linked to those on other sites. If you were less cynical (or making money from the company), you might conclude that this is based on a more altruistic reason. Because Google knows how much of that video the individual watches, it can better rate the relevancy of videos it hosts. Either way, there's a simple solution. Get your video on YouTube even if you host it elsewhere. In coming years, we'll see companies forming around video SEO, just as they did traditional search (many were later acquired by agencies). There is indeed a science and an art to tagging and indexing videos to ensure the Google spiders are kind.

YouTube Is Getting Googly

YouTube, despite its dramatic Yahoo!-like advertisement takeovers, is taking on attributes of its Mother Google. YouTube is searched more than Yahoo! or MSN, and eye charts show that the search box gets visual attention versus the other navigational elements (videos, channels, subscriptions). And YouTube advertisers can now target video search just as they do on Google, using the same tools. Advertisers have moved surprisingly slowly to extend campaigns on YouTube. Given that an advertiser can target either by impressions or using Google's per-click bid model, it is odd that more spending hasn't moved to YouTube for this alone.

How to Get Your Video to Appear on Google

The preceding head promises a lot, but the reality is that it's not completely within your control. If your video satisfies the searcher, then you have a chance of ranking and sustaining. However, there are some basic steps you can take to greatly increase your odds of getting your video content indexed and ranked:

Upload to YouTube. Design videos with search in mind, and post them on YouTube. You may have video that serves this purpose, and it's buried on a DVD in your company's dusty file cabinet. I worked in the pharmaceutical industry, and I would guess that less than 1 percent of manufacturers' video content is on YouTube.

Upload to other sites. TubeMogul is a free site that allows video creators and publishers to post their videos across dozens of online-video sites. Obviously, YouTube is often the fastest and easiest way to appear on Google, but other sites (Metacafe, Dailymotion, Yahoo! Video) also effectively present video content to search engines. These video sites already have authority with search engines and the "weight" of the parent site can improve your video page ranking on Google and other search engines.

Optimize your web site for video SEO. Google and other search engines invest a great deal of money and time to crawl web sites for video content. However, the technical configuration and content of web sites can make this extremely difficult. Search engines need to know where to find videos on your web site, and a properly configured video site map or video MRSS feed can help. Ensure that you are current on the best practices of this field, or ask your agency or hosting provider what it's doing to optimize video for search.

Be smart with title and descriptions. If your video has unique terms for the title, description, and keywords, then you've increased your odds of success. Be selective, and go for targeted and long-tail keyword phrases. For instance, do not try to optimize a search for "digital camera"; rather, choose a narrowed-down phrase like "how to buy cheap video cameras." It's important to be consistent with your title, first words of your description, and the keywords. There is a trade-off, because a title that works for search may not be as compelling for a viewer. Other SEO best practices apply for video. For instance, you may choose to spell words incorrectly. You can add commonly searched terms like *how to*, *viral*, and *parody*. Be aware that the first terms you use in descriptions, titles, and tags are the most important.

Utilize the thumbnail. Create a or select a compelling thumbnail to increase the chances that someone clicks your video. This, along with the title, is a vital determinant of a video being seen. If your video addresses people's needs, they are more likely o engage with your content. They also may reference or embed your video on their web site or social media presence, which will also help you on search engines.

Be mindful of video quality. Your video should address the needs of those who are searching for answers. Ideally, you will acknowledge their needs early in the video, and answer their questions before attempting to sell yourself or your services.

Text content of video words matters. Search engines will increasingly crawl content surrounding the video and this includes more than the title, description, and tags. Consider providing a closed-caption manuscript of your video, as this will help search engines until they're better capable of translating voice to text. Where possible, place your videos on web sites with relevant text surrounding them. You may even use annotations (text placed over your video) to refer to important terms.

Build inbound links. When popular and relevant web sites link to your video using the phrase "Best restaurant in NYC," then it's more likely you will rise in search rankings for that term. In fact, in the mid-1990s, there were two cases that proved how people are able to manipulate this variable in what has become known as *Google Bombing*. Web sites linked to President George Bush's bio on Whitehouse.org as "miserable failure, so that the president was a top search result for those searching "miserable failure" on Google. Comedian Stephen Colbert titled his web site "greatest living American" and asked others to do the same. For a while, these techniques worked to increase views. Since then, Google has become wise to bombing, however inbound links remain an incredibly important device to garner better search engine rankings. These are interpreted as endorsements for your content by search engines, which especially favor links from very popular sites and blogs.

Timing is important. Michael Buckley's "What the Buck" show, and Phil DeFranco's vlogs (video blogs) benefit greatly from their regular content about topics being searched. Their recent videos are often seen between 500,000 to 1 million times, and they have some videos that are cash cows for certain subjects (garnering regular views that are in the multimillions). As I write, they're no doubt making a video about the Golden Globes, knowing that on Tuesday, people will return to work and be grazing for recaps. This timely content also serves as "link bait" to popular social-media sites that are looking for current videos about hot content. Topicality is important, and the best personal example I can provide is my 2009 Super Bowl "Best Commercials" video. It maintains a poor attention score, meaning that there were early drops relative to most of my videos, but I launched it before last year's Super Bowl game. It garnered 3 to 4 million views in the days after last February's game, and it's up to 7 million now. The GoDaddy bosom thumbnail doesn't hurt, either, but that's not helping the attention score. If you want to see women's breasts, you're not really interested in seeing a dad and his kid talk about the best ads. If I did a daily vlog about the hot terms I found on Yahoo! Buzz, I'm quite certain I could dramatically expand my daily views from 150,000 to 200,000, or even 500,000. Alas, I have neither the time nor the interest to do this. I'm guessing Buckley and Phil DeFranco scour many sites to find out what content people are searching each day.

Engagement is essential. Your video will place more highly on search engines if it is well viewed, top rated, commented on, and labeled as a favorite. You also have an advantage if your video has been posted longer (since it has had more time to rise). As a result, YouTube stars have an edge on the rest. Their active fan following moves them to the top of the most-viewed videos, and makes it easy for a new audience to discover them. This is one of the reasons I urge marketers to tap into the credible platform of a weblebrity instead of posting their own videos. If I upload the same video, with identical descriptions, to my "Nalts" channel as well as to a new channel, the former is more likely to rise on search engines. Many people attempt to replicate this by asking friends and family to award their videos with a five-star rating, choose it as a favorite, and comment on it. However, a few dozen people aren't as powerful as the thousands of active fans who rate their favorite creators five stars even before watching the full video.

Stay current. Video sites and search engines will get increasingly savvy at preventing people from gaming them for views and ensuring that searchers find the information they need. So, in time, videos using thumbnails with neon graphics (a hot trend) and bosoms (a timeless tactic) will not outrank relevancy. Ultimately, I expect YouTube to rank videos based, in part, on "attention scores." YouTube tracks the attention score of a video based on how long people watch the video relative to other videos of similar duration. I can't tell precisely how many people stopped watching at a specific moment (or the average view duration), but I can see where people lost interest, and I try to manage that by teasing the audience with video that comes later. If a video for a particular term has a high attention score, then Google or YouTube can correctly assume it was relevant to the searcher. I'd expect this to be as vital as transcribed text.

What Doesn't Work

Now, I will turn your attention to a few things that don't work, or at least will prove unsuccessful soon enough.

Spam and Robot Blogs. I'm finding lots of spam automatic blogs that are now embedding my videos and descriptions and hoping to trick Google into indexing them. This annoying technique is also fooling Radian6 and other social-media monitoring tools, which report this old content as new. Last week, I tried a "Nalts" search on Radian6 and was frustrated to see old video descriptions appearing as recent buzz about me. Maddening.

Trolling. I'm also constantly finding my name packed with other YouTube usernames in videos by people who naively hope that trick will work. Did it ever work? It's a good technique if you're mentioning a particular YouTuber, because we do tend to ego-surf for content that tags our names. But as soon as I see 12 other youber names next to or alongside mine, I know trolling has taken place.

Inappropriate Thumbnails. Fake thumbnails might artificially drive views, but the video will be penalized when the attention scores show Google the video duped its users.

Getting Video Indexed on Google

By Amit Paunikar, product manager[3]

Indexing video content presents some unique challenges, and if you have videos on your site, you're probably wondering how to make sure your videos [are] more discoverable through Google. We want video publishers to know that we've made it easier to submit your videos to Google. First, we've simplified the submission process for sharing your "site maps," which is how a web site provides its organizational structure to Google's

(Continued)

"spiders." Second, we also extended our Video Sitemaps support to include Media RSS feeds. You do not have to specify the Sitemap file type—we'll determine the type of data you're submitting automatically.

The more information you make available, the easier it is for us to crawl (index) your videos. Here are a few simple things you can include in your Sitemaps to make your videos easier to find:

1. Landing page URL: This is the page where the video is hosted. It's better to have a unique landing page for each video on your site.

2. Video thumbnail URL: Thumbnails provide a strong visual cue to the user. Your video thumbnail should be representative of a snapshot from the video, and should not be misleading in any way.

3. Title and Description: If these are accurate and descriptive, they not only help Google understand your video, but also help users choose the best video search result. Providing information about category, keyword tags, and duration is always helpful.

Whether or not you have Video Sitemaps or MRSS feeds, of course, it's important that you make sure that Google can crawl and index your video sites correctly. Make sure you understand how Google crawls, indexes and serves the Web. Review the Webmaster Guidelines that will help Google find, index, and rank your site. We've also updated the Google Video Help Center to include more information for video publishers. While there's no guarantee that our spiders will find a particular site, following these guidelines should increase the chances of finding videos from your site in the search results.

The Eternal Delay of the Video Search Engine

Although YouTube is the second-largest search engine (after its parent, Google),[4] there is still no true video search engine. YouTube searches only its own content, and Google serves videos in its results, but video search lacks the sophistication of text search. In the years ahead, we will likely see Google indexing videos with help from advanced speech and text recognition technologies, and even image and facial recognition software.

Still, the leading video-sharing sites (YouTube and Hulu) have business models that increasingly limit their ability to act as complete video search engines. YouTube became popular, in part, because of its Google-like speed in finding television clips that were getting offline buzz, but copyright-law enforcement is weakening its influence. Hulu, by contrast, lacks the search sophistication of Google/YouTube and is meant for meals, not snacks. If you're searching for a short moment from a recent episode of *Saturday Night Live*, you may need to sit through long pre-roll ads in order to get to it.

Neither Hulu nor YouTube is sufficiently indexing videos hosted elsewhere, even when this may satisfy searchers. In fact, it's not in either web site's financial interest to index other sites. This opens the door for a neutral video-search engine that focuses not on where or how the video is served, but only on finding the best results. It is likely that Google will solve for this based on its accumulated knowledge of search nuances, but searchers may perceive a bias based on its ownership of YouTube.

In the past several years, YouTube facilitated "instant video on demand," for recently discussed television clips. For instance:

- After Tom Cruise danced on Oprah's couch, you could find footage on YouTube within hours.

- Want some context of an election quote? Find video of the entire speech instantly on the Internet.

- Miss America says something stupid? Search for it on YouTube.

In the past year, quick searches such as these have become more difficult because:

- Google/YouTube is not just passively flagging videos, but proactively screening or killing the most viral moments (they're usually copyright infringements that are ripped from television and posted by individuals who don't own the content).

- The ripped clips have been killed increasingly faster in recent months and years, but their online presence often lasts long enough to satisfy our need for instant gratification (24 hours or so).

- A clever YouTube searcher could, until recently, simply filter results by "today" and "most viewed" or "most recent" and find a clip in a few seconds—that is, before frustrated copyright owners yanked the ripped clips from the public domain.

Because Google inadvertently biases YouTube videos, there remains no adequate, neutral search engine for indexing video. In time, of course, we'll see an improvement in how "spiders" of Google and other search engines are able to "crawl" and index video content, and web sites will be better equipped to identify video content for the search engines.

CHAPTER 13

How to Get Popular on YouTube

In this chapter, you will learn:

- What helps video creators achieve popularity, and how that may apply to your own business, passion, or charity.

- How to create videos that engage viewers and increase the chances that they'll share your videos with others.

- What techniques are effective for attracting and sustaining viewers, and what gimmicks and black hat techniques can be counterproductive.

- Ways to promote your videos via blogs, web sites, and social media.

A popular YouTube video creator consciously or unconsciously practices many of the same behaviors in online-video creation as a good marketer does when selling a product. So, whether you are chasing fame on YouTube or not, you will gain new insight from insider secrets on developing a following on YouTube. This chapter is based on a free e-book titled "How to Become Popular on YouTube

Without Any Talent," which I first distributed in 2008. It is primarily devoted to video creators seeking wide global views, but does not address black hat techniques or tricks that ultimately undermine a creator. The focus is on often nonintuitive, but proven, strategies for developing and sustaining an audience.

While revising said e-book, I was surprised to find some e-mails while searching for feedback from the initial version. Among them was this note, sent from Shay Butler on January 1, 2008:

> *You are a true genius! I'm not just saying that. I just read all 34 pages of your book and LOVED it. I'm very new to YouTube, and waiting to gain 10,000 subscribers so I can celebrate [he's now got hundreds of thousands]. I'm addicted to this damned thing called YouTube. I have been looking for something exactly like your book this whole time. Thanks for being a YouTube mentor. Official Shaycarl book rating is three thumbs up! Since I only have 2 thumbs that's pretty dern [sic] impressive!*

ShayCarl has hundreds of thousands of subscribers and viewers, and has far eclipsed me with videos of his life, wife, and family, and I would be happy if I could take 2 percent of the credit (which I can't).

These techniques are built on experience, and will help you avoid some of the many pitfalls and violations of the unwritten rules of the YouTube community. They'll also save you from wasting time with ineffective approaches, and hopefully help you persist and have fun along the way.

If you're asking yourself the following questions, this chapter may be for you:

- How do I gain YouTube popularity without cheating or appearing desperate? What works, and what might create a backlash?

- What can I do to get my videos more views without spending an inordinate amount of time promoting them to people?

- How can I help make my videos viral (get them passed along)?

- How can I use my YouTube fame to promote myself, friends, advertising sponsors, or worthy causes?

Your primary goal is to have fun with this medium, which may create a loyal following and help you promote yourself or other causes. In general, I find three shared characteristics of the most-viewed YouTube stars: They enjoy making videos; they persist; and they are talented. The former two traits are as important as talent itself, and when someone stops having fun or becomes undermined by criticism, the talent itself serves little value.

You are, in fact, going to need some talent. But contrary to conventional wisdom, talent is not the only ingredient for success. In fact, there are far more talented people than me on YouTube who live in obscurity and deserve to have my incredible audience. But they're lost in a sea of garbage, maybe because they don't understand how to market themselves, and this may very well lead them to believe they're not so talented after all. It's sad, really.

Here's an important takeaway, so you might want to highlight this paragraph. YouTube fame (f) is a function of your talent (t) multiplied by your marketing (m): $f = t \times m$.

I really should stay as far from mathematical examples as I do from sports analogies. But this is vital. If you're a 9 out of 10 in talent, and this chapter takes you to a 5 (out of 10) in marketing yourself, then you're a healthy 45 overall. But if you're really not interesting (say, a 2 out of 10), then this chapter may not help much. Sorry.

I will touch briefly on how to make your videos *not* fail, but I've seen some extremely naive people on YouTube. I shudder to think that one of them is turning to this chapter for salvation. Not to be as obnoxious as Simon Cowell, but if your friends and family find your videos lame, then you may want to take up another endeavor.

Still reading? Great. If you take nothing else away from reading this, please remember this: The act of uploading is only one tiny step on your YouTube adventure, and if you stop there, you're not going to get very far.

Glossary of Terms

I use some terms in this chapter that are worth defining.

Collab Videos: Making a collaboration video with someone else on YouTube. This is an important way to introduce yourself to the YouTube community; it can be time-consuming, but it is also fun.

Subscribers: You know how your magazines magically show up in your mailbox? Hardcore YouTubers wake up each day and check their subscriptions. If they've subscribed to you, they'll know each time you post a new video. You want to shoot for quality, and not just quantity, of subscribers because they're the ones who will rate your videos. If they like what they see, your video will get honored and appear on some of the "most viewed" or "most discussed" lists, which gets you a secondary audience.

Honors: Temporary status a video garners if it's the most-viewed, most-discussed, or highest-rated video of a certain time period. A video receiving these honors will, temporarily, be placed on lists and be more likely to surface on a YouTube search.

Partner: YouTube shares advertising revenue with *Partners*. (To learn more, see YouTube's Partner Program page.) For most Partners, this income is not life changing, but it's nice to receive annuities based on the advertising that appears around your videos. Unlike when I first distributed "How to Become Popular on YouTube Without Any Talent," I now know a dozen people who are living full-time on YouTube Partner income.

Do You Really Want to Be a YouTube Star?

Let's evaluate YouTube "fame" for a moment, and make sure you really want what you're apparently after. I find most people in pursuit of YouTube weblebrity status are looking for one of four things:

1. They're performers looking for a stage.

2. They're looking to sell a product or service.

3. They're trying to fill a self-esteem void with positive feedback, ratings, and views (therapy is cheaper in the long run).

4. They're hoping to connect with similar people and share experiences.

I'm going to start by tempering your desire. You see, if you enter YouTube with desperation for fame, people are going to find you really annoying. You'll give off a scent like those people selling Amway at neighborhood picnics. You might even irritate people more than I do at times.

YouTube popularity is not all it's cracked up to be. You'll find yourself spending inordinate amounts of time on the site, you'll lose a great deal of your privacy, and you'll get insulted in ways you've never imagined possible.

Each day you'll feel guilty because you're ignoring someone's cry for help—"Watch my video," "Mention my sick friend," "Participate in my 'collaboration' video," "Tell me what you think of my son's video." Soon, your e-mail inbox will feel like a portal to hell—with desperate and thirsty souls screaming for just a drop of water, which only you can dole out.

In some ways, YouTube fame brings all of the negative aspects of actual stardom without the money and perks. You'll almost certainly become addicted, and sometimes you will fail to differentiate between your own view of yourself and the opinions of your viewers. The first time you get featured, or have a video that goes viral, a mad rush of adrenaline will fill you up, which will be followed by a crash akin to a drop in sugar levels.

But enough psychobabble. I just want you to realize there are some downsides to being a webstar. Now, let's explore the fun things you're going to experience if you have at least some talent and deploy the techniques you're going to learn here.

There are some fantastic perks to having an established audience for your videos. First, you'll meet some terrific people. I started online video in December 2005 with the naive hope of supplementing my income. I certainly wasn't in pursuit of meeting virtual friends, as I was busy enough with my day job and family. I do well enough neglecting my nonvirtual friends, much less forgetting the birthdays of my virtual ones. But I've met some really amazingly creative and interesting people on YouTube. Some are passing relationships, where you e-mail or mention each other in an occasional video. Others I have met in person to shoot videos, grab a drink, or huddle together with at YouTube gatherings that make Star Trek conventions look cool.

I've been brought to tears by videos made by my friends, and gained new perspectives from individuals—from all over the planet—with whom I'd otherwise have no contact. And I've laughed until I could barely breathe. Lately, I've leveraged my YouTube experience to help marketers benefit from online video. But most gratifying is the joy of interacting with other creators, and getting instant feedback when I experiment with a new approach. Whereas I used to burden my dinner guests with my new videos, I can now post a video on YouTube, go upstairs and shower, and return to find hundreds of comments that tell me if the idea sank or sailed.

Understanding the YouTube Community

Did you know YouTube is more than a search engine for videos? It's actually a lively community, and until you understand and respect that community, you're not likely to be widely seen. Certainly, there are exceptions—I call them "one-hit wonders." Sometimes a video is so darned remarkable that it goes viral on its own merit. But please don't bet on that, because you have a greater chance of getting killed by a llama. Many of the most popular videos on YouTube never help the creator generate a regular following, so their next attempt is futile. Viewers are likely to follow certain stars and content providers (regular shows), while other providers are fun to watch but not compelling enough to follow via subscriptions.

If you're new to YouTube, you may want to imagine yourself walking into the high-school cafeteria. What's your body language saying?

- *Sit with me because I'm afraid to sit alone.*

- *I came to eat, so please stay away or I'll eat you.*

- *Hi. I'm a cheerleader. Want to sit with me and be popular?*

- *Where's the table for the people who hate everyone else here?*

Because YouTube is a visceral medium with two-way interaction, you can't simply post your video and return a few days later to see if you're the next one-hit wonder. People are going to talk back to you eventually. If you listen and respond, they might stick around and watch more. They may even tell their friends about you. But if you're posting to YouTube like you're sending out mass holiday letters, your community reputation will be poor.

There's a core group of YouTubers who hang out on live videoconference web sites, e-mail each other constantly, and interact with one another in various ways. You can learn a lot from this group, and they'll influence your YouTube reputation. If I had more time (and didn't derive social anxiety from live video), I'd be on Stickam.com, BlogTV, or other web sites hanging out with these people regularly. Of course, this makes more sense for an entertainer than a marketer, who wouldn't likely command a regular live audience.

As with any community, there are countless unwritten rules. To fit in, you'll have to watch a lot of videos and get a sense for them yourself. But I'll give you a quick rundown.

Nobody wants to admit this, but there's a subtle social ladder based on how many subscribers you have. It's rather repulsive, and I try not to look at the numbers. I find that creators' egos can unjustly enlarge as their subscribers grow, and I often prefer to hang with the less popular, more interesting people. But this social ladder is undeniably important.

For example, I get a lot of requests to collaborate with people who have no videos or subscribers, and it is a lot easier to ignore them than someone who has talent and a following. I know some famous YouTubers who simply won't collaborate with someone who obviously doesn't watch their videos. If you try to do a collaboration video with HappySlip, for example, before you know her—and have developed your own following—she's likely to ignore you. (She ignores me most of the time, too, but that's survival when you're blasted with 100 e-mails a day.) So initially, you need to interact with people who have as many subscribers as you, and find your own "pod" within YouTube. There are countless subcultures built around people and their friends, and this group stays with you like your freshman roommates (or the stink of garlic).

Some YouTubers leverage their talent (in music or graphic design) to create custom material that popular YouTubers can use. This makes us far more interested in helping these creators find their way to the top. I've had several musicians or artists provide custom content for me, and I like to return the favor.

Methods behind the Madness

If you're a scanner, here comes the important part. I like lists because they simplify things, and they are actionable. So let me jump right into some of the techniques that have helped me on YouTube. I'd also encourage you to watch a few videos and blog posts I've done on the subject of YouTube etiquette.

You would be reluctant to believe that I, one of the greatest violators of YouTube etiquette, would dare to write and especially to make a video on the subject. My video can be found on YouTube under "YouTube Etiquette." and in that video I do just as I am about to and describe the five main components of YouTube etiquette.

1. **Posting.** There's a term called *turd dropping*, which is the act of posting a video on YouTube and hoping that somehow the video will get views based on the sheer quality of the content. This may work for Barats and Bereta—a comedic duo who post infrequently but gain consistent views. I tried posting videos without engaging for about nine months and was very dissatisfied with the overall statistics, posters, viewers, and so forth. I strongly recommend that you become more active on YouTube or do *shout-out videos*, which are directed to top YouTubers.

2. **Watching.** This is also an integral part of YouTube etiquette but can be rather insufferable, especially when people post eight-minute video logs. I use something known to me as the three-fourths rule." I will play a video in its entirety, leave the room as it plays so as to not bore myself, rewind about three-fourths of the way back into the video, wait for something funny to

be said, and comment on it. This gives the illusion that I watched the video in its entirety. Try this and see how it works for you.

3. **Interacting.** People like to interact with the people they view, so be sure to read the comments and attempt to reply to as many as you can or feel comfortable with. Personally, I like to reply to comments but not direct messages because of the constant violation of YouTube etiquette. There are three questions in these messages that I receive a great deal: (1) What type of equipment do you use and how do you compress it? (2) Will you watch my videos? (3) Will you please subscribe to my channel? Each of these gets very old very fast.

4. **Collaborating.** Nothing works to propel you up the ladder of online video like collaborating on a video with someone who has already gained popularity. However, you do not want to be a "subscriber leech." These are the people who want to do a collaboration video with you just to take away some of your subscribers.

5. **Meeting Other YouTubers.** When meeting fellow YouTube creators, it is good know who they are and what videos they have made. When approaching a webstar, it's not wise to mention that person's most popular video. Instead, mention something obscure, and never assume that she has seen any of your videos.

I hope what you have learned here will not only make you a more polite YouTuber, but a more successful one, too. The bottom line is that YouTube is not just a video-sharing site; it's a community. The sooner you can understand how to function and thrive within this community, the faster you can begin to use it for your own financial gain.

Collaborate with Other YouTubers

There's probably nothing you can do on YouTube that has more impact than collaborating. Quite by accident, I began interacting with people and collaborating with other YouTube creators. That is when things began to change. Collaborations are a fun experience, and they also introduce you to the audience of the person with whom you collaborate. For example, when I collaborated on a video with a popular YouTuber, Renetto, and he shaved my head to look more like his head, I got some exposure to his rabid fans. When I stalked HappySlip's New York City apartment, she was kind enough to post my video on her blog, and suddenly some of her subscribers subscribed to me. If you collaborate with someone whose content is similar to yours, this is more likely to occur.

I overlooked something critical in the first version of this "How to Become Popular on YouTube Without Any Talent." If you want people to discover you and your videos, it's more important that you are in the video of a popular YouTuber (versus having them in yours). Generally, a collaboration video is more valuable to the individual with the lowest number of subscribers.

TheStation, a relatively new collaborative channel, rocketed overnight to one of YouTube's most-subscribed because of the collective promotion by a number of YouTube stars, including Sxephil, ShayCarl, ShaneDawson, and LisaNova. ShayCarl, who was a stranger when I first published the e-book, is viewed exponentially more times than me. He first "popped" when Sxephil told his viewers to subscribe to Shay, and now ShayCarl has one of the most active fan bases on YouTube.

Pursue Quality Subscribers (Not Quantity)

Obviously, many of the people who subscribe to my videos on YouTube don't check the page that shows recent videos of those to whom they have subscribed. Others have lost interest in YouTube. But among these subscribers, there are people who share my sense of humor. Only a small portion people who graze YouTube actually subscribe to videos and check them routinely. But this core audience is vital, because they are the ones who will watch your videos, give you feedback, and rate you favorably. I'm able to post a video, and have it appear in YouTube's "most highly rated videos of the day" because I have a group of subscribers who generally like my stuff. Then, when other YouTube browsers search for the highest-rated videos of the day, they're finding my videos—thanks to my loyal subscribers.

There are a few of us who live on these "most watched" and "most discussed" pages, and many of us aren't very talented. But our subscribers like us, and that propels us to *honors*, which give us access to a secondary audience. My videos almost always get honors because I have a quality base of subscribers. But if I suddenly inherited all of the subscribers of Smosh (two popular comedians), I would probably get destroyed. Some of them would like me, but an old, balding guy who drinks out of a coffee mug bearing his YouTube name would not amuse many of them. So it's the quality of the subscribers that you want, not just the quantity.

Be Patient

Those creators who posted on YouTube early (circa 2005) have a powerful advantage over the rest of us. They got in early, and they developed a regular fan base when the pickings were slim. Renetto and MrSafety are good examples, although only the latter has persisted. They're almost as lacking in talent as I am (I say this in jest), but they have established audiences who really enjoy their content. It's very hard for a newcomer to rank initially. Please remember, it's a marathon, not a sprint! Save some energy and pace yourself.

Interact

The YouTube audience is watching less television and becoming enthralled with online video because it's mostly real and amateur. Most of us are tired of scripted television, or worse yet, the faux reality television shows. Viewers want to see real people who are accessible and authentic, and with whom they can connect. This means you should try to read and reply to as many comments on each video as possible (and not just your own). This is easy at first, but becomes overwhelming as time goes on. Still, my favorite part of YouTube is the discussion that takes place on the video within the first 24 hours. I almost never check comments from old videos, but I tend to jump online to my most recent video and read and reply to interesting comments. If you ever want to catch the attention of a YouTuber, try commenting on his most recent video. The more popular the person is, the less likely he is to read YouTube messages or e-mail.

POST ROUTINELY

A year ago, my slogan, "Nalts posts a video every time you poop," was accurate.

But I soon received feedback that my videos were losing quality, and many people suggested I emphasize quality over quantity. I listened, and it was a tremendous mistake. Soon I was posting as infrequently as 10 times per month, and it reduced my momentum dramatically.

I now do my best to post routinely, and it's a critical component to my success. The video creators who currently top the charts have one thing in common: They post frequently and, in most cases, daily. This does not mean that posting regularly will propel you to fame, but once you're on top, it's important to keep your edge and stay "top of mind" to those who watch your videos. Unlike my early days on YouTube, only a minority of my daily views come from subscribers or recent videos. People will more likely discover and view your videos if you're predictable about posting on specific days or times.

But if the quality occasionally suffers, could that alienate people? Consider Psychology 101. Humans tend to repeat a habit even when the rewards vary. Look no further than the neighborhood bar or casino to see examples of how we persist in a behavior even when the payoff is intermittent.

Going Beyond YouTube: "Seeding"

Remember that YouTube is the most popular video site and number one search engine, but it is only one place, of many, where YouTube videos are seen. When you post your video, you may want to market it on niche sites, blogs, and discussion groups. I tend to avoid this because it's time-consuming and, if not done carefully, it can violate communities.

For instance, when I did a video about my obsession with *The Office*, I resisted the temptation to send the link to those blogging about the show. Unless you devote the time to personalizing your note (as in the following format), then you're probably going to look like a spammer. That said, marketing your videos to blogs and social-media sites has helped many popular creators.

Here's an example of an e-mail I'm happy to get:

Dear Kevin: I've been reading WillVideoForFood .com for quite some time, and particularly enjoyed your recent post on [insert topic]. I work for a company that does [insert company description], and I would imagine this would be of some interest to your readers. Could I send you information for the possibility of being mentioned in a future post?

Contrast that with a random comment (including a link) on my blog from a promoter or public relations flack. As a blogger about online video, I am inundated with e-mails about campaigns or video contests. These feel like junk mail to me—at best, you'll get some moderate uptake.

There are countless social-media vehicles that can help you promote your videos (MySpace, Friendster, Facebook, Digg). I find these overwhelming and not nearly as productive as my other techniques, but other YouTubers swear by the power of these. A good resource on this subject is CharlesTrippy's "Viral Video Fever."

My best personal example of the impact of *seeding* videos to blogs and web sites is the success of my parody of the MacBook Air. When I received an e-mail from Apple that announced the slick new product, I spent 20 minutes shooting a video that depicted my PC feeling insecure about being overweight. I called it: "MacBook Air Obsessed With

Thin" (which I later changed to "MacBook Air Parody" to optimize it for search engines).

Just before going to sleep, I sent the video's URL to a few Mac blogs. Gizmodo (a very popular blog) posted it, and it was quickly discovered by tens of thousands of people. Obviously, the video's topicality helped, and it's now approaching 700,000 views.

A little "blog gasoline" on the "video spark" is well worth its time.

BE HOT

I asked for feedback on my first e-book, and a viewer named Yuri from New Zealand wrote: "I've seen people with no talent at all with YouTube partnership. . . . Is it about looks? You did state that YouTube is the same as the first day of school and I noticed that usually popular kids are more handsome or pretty."

I wish I could tell Yuri that looks don't matter, but they do. Many of the most popular YouTube creators are attractive-looking. Pretty females have a higher likelihood of success than a middle-aged guy like me. But there are exceptions, and I can't quite envision Sxephil, ShayCarl, or KassemG on the cover of GQ.

I truly believe that energy, body language, positive attitude, and humor are core drivers. In the early days of YouTube, there were many surly vloggers. Today, many of the most-viewed webstars are fun people who have viewers who consider them as friends.

Avoid These Tricks at All Costs

There are ways to artificially drive the views and ratings of your videos, and tricks you can use to spam your videos to others. Ultimately, these won't help much because you'll lose credibility and annoy people. It's cheap, tacky, and may give you a short-term boost, but it's just not worth the effort.

Here are some other mistakes I've seen people make as they try to popularize their videos. Maybe you can save yourself some time and humiliation by reading this list.

BLATANT-SELF-PROMOTION

I often get accused of blatant self-promotion because YouTube began as a community site for open dialogue, and I'm a marketer. I can't resist a logo, a token hat, and a Nalts logo mug that sneaks into a frame with all the subtlety of a migraine. Perhaps subconsciously some of my self-promotional behavior is driven by a desperate attempt to gain popularity to fortify my self-worth. But a lot of what I do is meant as a self-deprecating humor. It's also fun to annoy people.

Still, self-promotion can go terribly wrong. I wish I could show you some of the desperate e-mails I get requesting me to gratuitously mention someone else so they can get famous. I get many requests to be in collaboration videos when the creator has no audience of his own, nor any idea of what he is trying to do (other than to borrow some fame). It's awkward and embarrassing. Most of the popular YouTubers are insecure people with no experience with fame, so they are inconsistent about what collaborations they join. Desperation for fame is, in general, a turnoff, and something to avoid at all costs.

SPAMMING

Unless there's a good reason to send people a video, let them find it on their own. For instance, I almost never send someone a link to my recent video (except, of course, my mom) unless they're mentioned or in it. There's nothing for the ego like getting invited to watch a video in which you make a cameo or you're referenced. But I stopped reading my YouTube mail because 90 percent of the messages were:

- What type of equipment do you use? (I explain that in my profile page.)

- Will you watch my video and tell me what you think? (No specific reason—just a desire to be seen by a popular stranger?)

- You are so incredibly sexy. (Okay—that's not one I've received before, but I wanted to make sure you're still awake!)

There are other forms of spamming videos through social networks and *friends* lists, and candidly, I don't even understand most of these. LisaNova (one of the most popular YouTube comedians) faced severe backlash for apparently spamming people via YouTube to promote her videos. She made a public apology on the subject, as well as a parody that now has millions of views. The bottom line is that your videos should be viral based on the content and some promotion, but not through lazy and automated ways that will simply annoy people.

Also, stay away from the fee-based promotional tools that are done by software, which are typically scams.

DON'T KEYWORD-BLOAT

When an individual uploads a video, she can include a description and keywords (tags) that help people and search engines find the content. Many people have a naive belief that if they bloat their keywords with terms like *funny*, *humor*, *comedy*, and even names of popular YouTube personalities, it will propel the video to the top of a related search. Indeed, this myth is not without some basis of truth. Keywords not only help people find the video, but they can propel it to the top of Google and ensure it appears beside related content on YouTube.

When I was first featured on YouTube, however, I noticed that people were posting their videos as replies, and mimicking my video's keywords. This is misleading and annoying, and will eventually penalize a video's performance. Remember: YouTube is now owned by the master of defying search-engine manipulation, Google.

A better approach is to use relevant keywords in hopes that your video appears beside related videos. It's not a bad idea to misspell, either. For example, sellers of Heelys shoes are spending massive advertising budgets to have their sites appear on the common misspelling of their brand. If you type in "Healies," my video (called "Poor Man's Healies") is unintentionally one of the top results, simply because I can't spell.

One of the most effective ways to ensure your video is optimized by search engines is to be selective about the terms or phrase you choose as keywords. The first words of your description and keywords should be competitive terms, and in general, shorter titles are preferable.

ABUSING "VIDEO RESPONSES"

YouTube allows you to reply to another video, and this is a functionality that is often abused. Many people tack their videos onto popular videos, knowing that bored peo-ple will click them out of curiosity. Some video creators police this vigilantly by not allowing people to post replies without their approval. (They select a YouTube option that moderates video responses instead of permitting them auto-matically.)

I don't have time to groom the video replies, so I some-times let anything get posted. However, I become very annoyed when people post videos that have no relation-ship to mine, and I will occasionally block them (prevent them from interacting with me) as a result.

GETTING TOO SELF-CRITICAL

If you're frustrated because you aren't finding an audience, move past it. Focus on doing videos that make you happy, and give them time. If you begin to doubt yourself, your videos will get worse. And don't allow a few negative people to throw you off your course. Don't give negative viewers a voice. As Dori says in the Pixar film, *Finding Nemo*, "Just keep swimming!"

WAITING TO BE DISCOVERED

YouTube editors once had the most powerful jobs in modern media, and could literally turn obscure talent into overnight fame by simply featuring a video. Once, a YouTube community manager ("BigJoeSmith") brought me to the home page of YouTube by featuring "Viral Video Genius," but the video was only moderately well received. The second time I was featured on the web site was for my breakout video called "Farting in Public." I will confess, for the first time ever, that I sent this video to the editors. I only did that a few times because it felt self-serving and obnoxious to abuse it.

The videos that are sporadically featured, in what's called *spotlighting*, are mostly videos by YouTube Partners (visit www.youtube.com/partners to learn about this program). These videos are monetized with advertisements. Becoming a Partner is an important move, but then what is most important is *persistence*. As discussed earlier, this was a common theme among creators featured in a YouTube documentary, "I Want My Three Minutes Back." The film showed how creators vary in style and talent, but generally have persistence as a common trait.

INFRINGING COPYRIGHTS

Ensure your work is entirely your own, or that you have sufficient permission. Otherwise your content can be removed, and you will jeopardize your YouTube Partner status. Rather than using a popular song, find a talented amateur musician who might share his or her songs in exchange for a credit.

How to Make Videos You and Others Will Enjoy

Because I make so many videos, many of them are quite bad. If anyone should have the magic recipe for a good online video, it should be me. But I'm still learning each day, and that's part of what makes it so fun to create videos. People often ask me why I don't focus on creating fewer videos overall—with the extra time enabling better quality—instead of posting a mix of good and bad ones routinely. There are two reasons for that. First, if I stop creating for more than a few days, I generally don't feel like posting anymore. Second, it is not easy to predict exactly which videos will become popular. There are many factors involved, so I play the odds with volume and frequency. As I mentioned earlier, the unintended outcome of this routine posting is that it also keeps your audience loyal and aware.

That being said, there are a number of things I'd advise to help you make better videos. Technically, the barriers to entry are extremely low (access to the Web, a computer, and an inexpensive camera). But following are some tips to make your videos interesting and more likely to be shared, therefore giving them more potential to become viral.

Stick to Your Brand (Be Yourself)

I know that my videos might be more popular if I made them more edgy and sexy. But it's not consistent with my style, and so I forgo that upside. It's not sustainable to create content that doesn't reflect your personality, and it will confuse your audience. Find a unique style and stay with it. That doesn't mean you shouldn't experiment. Some of the best YouTube creators have a very specific and *ownable* style. Michael Buckley does daily celebrity gossip with the "What The Buck" show. Smosh does sketch comedy. HappySlip makes clever comedies about her home life that also express her musical talent, among other things.

These creators aren't just talented; they know their audiences and consistently provide for them. Some, of course, participate more extensively with the YouTube community, and others have their eyes toward larger media opportunities. To see other popular YouTubers, visit the "most subscribed of all time" section and get a feel for what's out there. Just resist the temptation to imitate these styles too closely. Find your own niche.

I tend to prefer variety in my videos—from simple vlogs (talking directly to camera) and real family moments to sketch comedy and *Candid Camera* style–videos. I've even done suspense and thriller style, but usually with a comedic element. When "Farting in Public" was featured, I picked up thousands of new subscribers, and some of those stuck around. Others left disappointed that all of my videos weren't in the same candid style.

In writing this book, I asked a number of popular video creators what advice they would give to fellow creators. Many of them encourage others to "find their own voice" and ensure that it's unique.

SHORT, FAST, AND BIG FINISH

There are no hard rules about making a video, and many videos fail because they try to replicate other viral videos. People generally want short play time (one to three minutes or less), rapid editing, and a big finish.

Sometimes I break this rule, but it's a basic tenet of short-form video on the Internet. It is almost always better to keep video shots between 30 and 90 seconds, even if it prolongs the editing process. When you're editing, you sometimes can't resist keeping some footage. Sometimes when I return to a video weeks after posting, my undisciplined editing infuriates me. The viewers will never miss that gag that extended your video from two to four minutes, and you'll find your views are inversely related to the length of your videos. If you must tell the story in more than two to three minutes, consider breaking it into a three-part series.

I sometimes overlook the power of the big finish, but it truly is the magical moment.

If people lose interest or lack excitement at the end, they won't forward the video to others. If there's a great ending, however, viewers will forgive some of the dips in the middle. And they'll rate it higher and share it with others. Surprise them at the end, or at least return to a previous gag so the story doesn't taper away.

There's nothing I enjoy more than finalizing the editing of a video, and adding music. It helps to have someone watch your video with you, and note when they look bored. I've chopped my videos down by watching my wife's blank stare when I preview them to her. You'll sense what you can lose. Sometimes the best part of the video is what you decide to leave out.

DON'T OBSESS OVER PRODUCTION QUALITY

Want to know a secret? Many top creators have lousy equipment. For instance, the wonderful MediocreFilms promotion for a yearbook printer was shot on a flipcam. The GooTube Conspiracy trailer was shot on a low-end camera using an antiquated computer processor. Many of the people dominating the most-popular YouTube videos each day are using simple flipcams. If you want good tips on equipment check Steve Garfield's blog. For software, check Chris Pirillo's.

A mediocre video can become much more appealing if the creator worries less about fancy equipment and more about the lighting, camera angles, editing, and sound. Many people gravitate to online video because they're tired of overproduced television and film. You're allowed to have a wobbly camera and some rough editing. However, there are some basic tips—and countless web sites dedicated to the topic—that can help you improve your production:

- Light your subject softly with lights on two sides (not ceiling lights that produce a shadow). Natural light (overcast) produces the best quality.

- When possible, use an external microphone, and avoid public places with ambient sound and horrible acoustics. Most YouTube creators use the microphone on the camera, which is usually poor. There's nothing that screams amateur like the echo of a room.

- Edit tightly so no shot lasts more than five seconds. The best movies have rapid-fire editing, and short-form entertainment needs the same treatment.

PACKAGE YOUR VIDEO

Your video encompasses more than the video. Your thumbnail, description, title, and even keyword tags on the videos are part of the package. If these elements aren't consistent with your video idea, the video won't have the same impact.

Some creators work hard for a good thumbnail, which is the image that appears besides the video title. YouTube once drew these images by default from the exact center frame of the video (so a two-minute video would use the image that appears at exactly one minute), or the first or last third of the video. Now, the thumbnail is randomly chosen unless you are a YouTube Partner and have the ability to upload an image that becomes your thumbnail. Lately, some of the top YouTube talent has been using bright, neon colors with a simple image (often the webstar's face) over it.

Using a photo of an attractive woman in this thumbnail, which certainly works in the short term, has penalized some YouTubers. Many of the curiosity clicks will result in frustrated viewers who were expecting something else. In general, the video's thumbnail is one of the most important drivers of views.

The title of your video also plays a significant role in the decision of a subscriber to watch it. I sometimes change my titles when I think of stronger ones. For example, the video I posted this morning features Spencer, the boy from "Farting in Public," beating up his friends with a huge inflatable soccer ball and basketball. The title is "Spencer Has Big Balls." That should arouse some curiosity. In general, good titles are short and increase curiosity in the viewer.

Conclusion and Summary

If you began this chapter to propel yourself to fame, I hope you've realized that there are effective strategies and some hidden pitfalls. More important, I hope you realize that there is tremendous gratification that comes along the way. I hope you'll focus on the fun of the journey, and not just on the destination of fame. You'll be criticized like never before, but you'll also get wonderful feedback and meet fantastic people. And occasionally, you'll find out you've made someone else's life better, or at least a bit more interesting.

There are other important video sites, but I've focused mostly on YouTube because it's the low-hanging fruit, and currently where the vast majority of videos are seen. If you can crack the YouTube code, you can always explore other sites. The audiences between these sites overlap less than you'd think. I use TubeMogul to upload my videos to a dozen sites, but few get anywhere near the number of views that I get on YouTube.

CHAPTER 14

Can You Make Money from Online Video?

In this chapter, you will learn:

- Why most video start-ups have failed.

- How to make money via online video if you're willing to invest time.

- What video content will engage your audience instead of making them feel "pitched."

- About another attempt at the Web-studio model that may work—or not.

Reality Check

There have been countless companies attempting to cash in on the growth of online video, and most have failed. When I began covering the space in 2005, there were dozens of online-video sites, and several that shared revenue with creators (Revver.com and Metacafe.com as the pioneers). As with almost any other industry, a dominant player emerged in YouTube, and most of the other web sites eventually folded. The market can sustain multiple search engines, but we tend to prefer one or two primary video or social-media sites. The video sites were reaching people, but the advertising revenue dollars to subsidize them has been slow to migrate from television and print.

Likewise, there have been countless attempts at creating a Web studio, which would produce online-video series with the funding of investors or sponsors. However investors are weary given online video's unproven economics—most consumers expect it for free, and advertisers are still "dipping their toes" in the medium. Even worse, many of the potential Web studios expect advertisers to bankroll a show that has not yet found an audience online.

The fundamental problem with the new studio is that even a cost structure that is modest by comparison to television is still cost-prohibitive for online video at this stage. The audience is growing, but not yet sufficiently around professional content. Online media buyers are reluctant to spend without guarantees of reach. So there's a catch-22 for larger players that does not exist for us webstars. A webstar's costs are low, and he or she sets out to please an audience with almost no revenue for years. Eventually, individuals find income from YouTube's Partner Program and the occasional sponsor. The income for a recent college graduate is not trivial, but it's not sufficient for a family of six. Similarly, it's not enough to cover a staff of writers, cameramen, editors, promoters, and agents (and certainly not real estate in New York City).

I am often asked to speak on the subject of online monetization, and my advice is simple:

1. **Keep it cheap.** A production doesn't need to be expensive to garner an audience, and highly produced content has not yet proven to be more attractive to the online-video community. That may

change, but I cringe when I hear Web studios taking pride in "$1,000 per minute" productions. That means your two-minute video better yield $2,000 of income, and I'm willing to bet it won't.

2. **Amplify.** There is no prime time in online video. So the time spent getting a video seen may outpace the time creating a video. That can be done efficiently through social media, seeding content to bloggers, and creative partnerships. A word of caution, however: It's almost cost-prohibitive to advertise a video that depends on advertising revenue for income.

3. **Listen.** Online video is not yet distribution; it's dialogue. Video creators should listen to their audiences and engage in a dialogue. Overproduced content and repurposed trailers or advertisements are not going to have the same impact as a person speaking to an audience directly and listening to that audience. Many professional producers underestimate these nuances, and consider their work done when their show is submitted.

4. **Find the crowd.** "Fish where the fish are" is perhaps the most overused colloquialism of the medium, so let's use a film model. Would you rather debut your film in a community cinema or via Regal, AMC, or Loews? Eventually, Apple or Microsoft may generate audiences, and perhaps Hulu will sustain them. Cable television may also find a way to preserve its stronghold. But today you're on YouTube or you don't exist—in the online-video realm.

5. **Fill a content niche sought by advertisers.** The YouTube Partner Program, while significant for those with at least 1 million views a month, is not

sufficient for most video creators. The better long-term model is to find a niche with unmet needs (moms, cooks, chess players) and create video content they love. Once you have a loyal following, you're in an excellent position to attract sponsors. This approach is far easier than asking marketers to subsidize your content and support it with their social-media marketing budgets.

YouTube and Cash

I should not begrudge those hoping to make money on YouTube—considering that revenue was an initial motivator for me. I do find it curious that people flock to YouTube in hope of making quick profits when there appear to be other, more proven ways to make money online (perhaps selling vitamins or white papers). Indeed, I have dozens of friends who are now making a full-time living on YouTube advertising revenue, and earning far more than they could in their previous professions.

Visitors to my blog, WillVideoForFood, most often arrive after searching Google for phrases like "How much money YouTube Partners make," or "How to make money on YouTube." So I would be remiss not to include some content on that topic specifically.

YouTube shares advertising revenue with those who meet requirements as YouTube Partners. The company's criteria is published, but not consistently applied (and can vary over time, or by who reviews the application). In general, your videos have to be your own (no copyright infringements), they need millions of views, and you should have a steady history of posting. If you apply and are not accepted, try again after you have amassed more views.

As I mentioned, I started in online video with hopes of entertaining people as well as supplementing my income. Initially, I made a few thousand dollars total through sites like Revver and Metacafe, which shared advertising revenue. However, I found this to be very, very slow money. I am not allowed to disclose my income from the YouTube Partner Program, but, in general, it's "life changing," although not significant enough to be my sole source of income.

That said, YouTube webstars are making a full-time living from the combination of YouTube Partner revenue and sponsored videos. If you lack an internal desire to create videos, and your primary goal is to make money, there are far more productive alternatives. For example, find a topic that has a high Google cost-per-click (litigation, mortgage, diet, digital cameras), and start a blog about it with Google AdSense ads sprinkled throughout.

Most popular video creators are driven first by other needs or desires (creative outlet, desire for attention, social interaction), and money comes as a welcome bonus. If I divided the revenue I've made from online video by the time I've invested, I would probably discover a job at Burger King would fetch a better hourly wage. However, I'm extremely grateful that online video has provided me with a secondary income. To some degree, the financial reward has damaged my appeal. Studies have shown that, counterintuitively, when money is introduced, creativity generally declines. Likewise, some of my audience has become fatigued with my frequent profit-driven promotions.

That said, it can be fun to make a video for a large brand and to help the company engage with the online community with far more relevance and impact than an online advertisement. I was one of several top YouTube Partners to be included in a General Electric campaign focused broadly on health, which accepted health challenges from viewers. That kind of program has benefits that are more significant than mere monetary gain.

If you seek YouTube popularity to market yourself or your products, I would recommend putting that goal aside until you develop a regular following. This is obviously easier for an entrepreneur or individual than it is for a large corporation.

The community will welcome you more if they don't see you as a walking advertisement. There are subtle ways to profit from your talents without looking like a sellout, whether you're a musician, painter, or voice-over professional. For instance, I've done several collaborations with Brett Slater (slatersgarage.com), and he uses his increasing online popularity to promote his voice-over and production services—without appearing overtly promotional.

The "New Studios"

A new breed of online-video studios has formed in recent years to meet the need for professional content in short-form video. Most have failed because few consumers are willing to pay for online-video content yet, and advertisers are only beginning to shift budgets to this medium. There's a more pervasive problem that caused this "pile of wreckage" (to use the words of Daisy Whitney in "Rethinking the Digital Studio," which follows). Many early attempts at Web studios were overengineered. Like television, they used large crews of writers, directors, editors, and actors. The surviving studios are tapping individuals with multiple production, editing, acting talent—known as "backpack producers" or "preditors" (producers and editors). What this model loses in quality it more than offsets in speed and efficiency.

As an example, I met recently with the people behind T180 studios, a digital entertainment studio owned by Disney. The company found Devon Kelly, who hosts "Electric Spoofaloo" via a Craigslist advertisement, and Kelly serves a variety of roles beyond performer.

When I met with Chris M. Williams, T180's general manager, to discuss a keynote presentation at his hotel in early 2010, he offered me a bottled water he purchased from a nearby Walgreens. Even the well-backed Web studios are being careful about spending.

Rethinking the Digital Studio

By Daisy Whitney

The pile of wreckage in the digital studio business is impressively high, littered both with venture-backed and network-owned in-house shops.

Given the history of the past years and given how very risky making content is in the first place, it seems a bit insane for a media company to start a digital studio today.

But history didn't stop Fox Television Studios from launching its new digital studio "Fox 15 Gigs." Finding the Web properties that can successfully make the leap to television is still the brass ring in Hollywood. There have been attempts, mostly notably *Quarterlife*, which famously failed when NBC launched the Web show as a midseason replacement two years ago.

(Continued)

The promise, though, of a Web-to-TV crossover show is so alluring that Hollywood creators like Fox keep trying. For example, 15 Gigs is housed within Fox Television Studios, the cable studio best known for USA Network's *Burn Notice*. The modus operandi of 15 Gigs is to use the Web as an inexpensive proving ground for concepts, ideas, and talent. The better ones to emerge from the Web stew could graduate to TV.

That's how 15 Gigs differs from predecessors like Disney-ABC's Stage 9, which launched in 2008 but laid off most staffers last year after its lackluster lineup of shows didn't take off. It's also a different beast than a pure-play digital studio like 60 Frames, which went under in 2009.

Because 15 Gigs isn't going after Web hits, its goal is simple—to use the Web to nurture ideas cheaply. Then the digital studio can call the best ones up to the Major Leagues of TV, because that's where the big bucks still are. As an example, 15 Gigs is currently pitching its successful online series, *When Ninjas Attack*, as a *Wipe-Out*–style game show for network TV.

"Most of the stuff we have done is done for less than the cost of a script," said Gabriel Marano, VP of programming at Fox Television Studios.

Another distinction is 15 Gigs doesn't operate alone. "We aren't a network. We're just one of the studios here at Fox, and we feel 15 Gigs is an extension of our development process," said Ilsa Berg, director of programming at Fox Television Studios. "We can produce a web series cheaply, and once you get it on tape you can see if you even want to do the rest of the series. It's not that different from what we do as a studio every day. You need to make things in a cost-efficient way."

That includes looping in advertisers. Marano said 15 Gigs is pursuing branded entertainment deals and that it expected to have inked advertiser partnerships by late last year. The studio also works closely with Fox Digital Media on digital strategy, sales, and marketing.

"It's not meant to be a deficit-financed idea," Marano said. "Right from the get-go there is a vision of how to be profitable, such as partnering with the right distribution platform where it's ad supported, where ad dollars are high enough value, and where advertisers are brought on board."

As part of its incubation approach, the digi-studio inked a development deal with Web producers Black20. The creative shop is best known for edgy comedic videos as well as regular web series like *The Middle Show*. Collectively, Black20's videos have earned 60 million views. Now, the Web creators are working with 15 Gigs to test ideas for possible TV development.

Black20 is a good fit for the ultra-low-cost model at 15 Gigs. With just nine employees in Queens and only $500,000 in angel funding, Black20 has learned to produce on a shoestring. Black20 also relies on multiple revenue streams, earning money by producing promos for cable networks, creating video series for portals like IGN.com and via its own ad deals with Colgate, Loopt, and others.

Also, 15 Gigs has another Black20-style development deal in the works and is aiming to be the go-to development studio for creative talent that knows how to leverage the Web, Marano said.

(Continued)

Still, any digital studio faces inherent challenges, pointed out Keith Richman, CEO of Break Media, which produces Web videos and commands a distribution network reaching more than 60 million unique visitors each month.

"I think the challenge they will have is no different than any other digital studio: They lack distribution online, which makes monetization difficult. Alternately, if their goal is just to pilot stuff and test the content for television, the challenge is that scripted episodic content has not done great online at any mass scale," he said.

Marano pointed out that 15 Gigs videos are distributed on Hulu and YouTube, as well as on MySpace and FunnyorDie in many cases. But the digi-studio is platform agnostic, so its content can be pitched and sold to both its sister divisions, like the Fox networks, as well as Web portals and other places.

Plus, the "digital incubation" model has proven successful with others, such as multimedia studio Electric Farm Entertainment. "Introducing a franchise through low-cost digital platforms with the intent to slowly grow an audience and, in success, grow the franchise up the media food chain makes sense to me—it's the model Electric Farm and MTV used on Web series *Valemont*, which is now in consideration for becoming an on-air series," said Brent Friedman, one of the founders of Electric Farm.

A media company needs at least a three-year runway before it can take off for profitability, and that's the goal for the new video destination Take180.com.

The Disney-owned Web studio that specializes in spoofs and so-called participatory Web series launched in late March with three interactive series and is averaging about 1.5 million to 2 million views per month, said Chris M. Williams, Take180's general manager.

Already, Take180 has landed some ad support with parent company Disney's "G-Force" as one of the site's sponsors. Though the deal is with a sister company—the film studio arm of the corporate parent—Williams explained that Take180.com has to compete for those ad dollars just as any other site does. Take180.com, like most Web video destinations, is banking on advertising as its primary revenue stream.

Williams is betting on the interactive nature of the shows it produces as a key to winning advertisers. Most Take180 series give viewers the chance to participate in "challenges" by submitting videos that are often incorporated into the storylines of the shows, such as "Electric Spoofaloo," "My Date," and "I Heart Vampires."

"Media businesses need runways," he said. "If you're not giving a media business three years, you're not giving it justice, and you can't compromise audience growth for revenue early on."

CHAPTER 15

Guerrilla Video for Entrepreneurs and Cause-Related Marketing

Entrepreneurs or nonprofits generally lack agencies and large budgets, and are better suited to guerrilla marketing via online video. I would encourage small businesses or individual consultants to review Chapter 13, "How to Get Popular on YouTube," since the advice there is applicable to those with start-ups or cause-related marketing.

In this chapter you will learn:

- How to use online video and social media to garner intelligence about your marketplace.

- Ways to identify video-production talent without the high costs that large companies and agencies face, and distribute and promote that content on a shoestring.

- Techniques to help market your service, product, or cause via video webstars already speaking to your target audience.

- How to create your own videos to satisfy your customers' needs (for information or entertainment), and earn the right to promote.

Entrepreneur magazine reaffirmed the benefit to small business: "Going way beyond YouTube, online video has become a necessity among businesses and individuals looking to boost traffic and create a sophisticated web presence." If you're marketing yourself, or your products or services, online video can be a complement to paid search for efficiently targeting prospects.

Finding Talent

The reality is that there's a lot of amateur talent available to work without high costs—often individuals who work part-time or who are students. They can create incredible videos, brilliant graphic design, and understand social media. Those marketing without agencies and large budgets can benefit from tapping these skill sets on an ad hoc basis. Unfortunately, there's not yet a sufficient matchmaker between these entities, although some web sites (eLancer) do exist. For example, Poptent.org has thousands of independent creators who are available to create polished video content. The creators and directors often don't have an audience, but they can create online-video advertisements or branded entertainment for a fraction of typical production studio costs.

Ben Relles, when he first conceived "Obama Girl," placed an ad for directors on Craigslist, and within hours had reels from a variety of independent creators without the cost structure of production studios.

Going Direct to Webstars

Since small companies may lack resources to commence an integrated campaign with Google or engage with a company like Hitviews (which, again, helps identify webstars and leverage their reach without paid advertising), there is a more complex but efficient alternative. Entrepreneurs or charities may opt to identify talent on their own, and offer money or products in exchange for product placement or sponsorship. For instance, a seller of jewelry may discover a popular YouTube artist. The retailer may purchase her products in exchange for the YouTube artist to promote the store. There are many people on YouTube with moderate audiences (10 to 50,000 subscribers) who would be happy to promote a video camera if they received a free one from a manufacturer. Even clothing manufacturers could choose to send YouTube webstars free outfits to increase the visibility of the product. In general, my friends on YouTube (even those who receive millions of views per month) don't receive free products from companies, and they would welcome the exchange. In return, the creator is likely to plug the product or at least thank the company. This works less effectively with top webstars who may be fetching $5 to $15,000 per sponsored video. These individuals don't want to commercialize their channels without higher compensation.

Humanizing Your Venture

I typically urge start-ups and nonprofits to find a charismatic person to create regular videos and engage with the community. While this requires some time, it helps personalize the venture and can engage new audiences. For instance, our neighbor runs an animal rescue called Animal Lifeline. I've done numerous videos to increase awareness of her charity, and it has helped her fund-raising efforts. I once auctioned off a $2 stapler I had stolen from the apartment of

Christine Gambito (HappySlip). Christine also sent an autographed photo of herself, and someone bid $800 to benefit the charity.

These activities help humanize a company or cause, and extend messages far beyond what is possible through a web site. They also provide direct benefits in the area of search engine optimization.

The Poor Man's Search Engine Optimization

Video works especially well if you market a very unique product, and want to appear on search engines without significant cost. For instance, a local company, Byers Choice, sells collectable dolls, and has a specific product line that is designed for antique automotive enthusiasts. Its web site would not likely index high on a Google search for something like "antique dolls for automotive enthusiasts" or "gifts for car lover," but a video with those titles has a chance of a first-page search result. The cost of creating the video could be nominal (a few minutes using a $100 video camera and a few more minutes to upload and tag the video). If it generated just a few sales, it would more than offset the investment.

Social-Media Monitoring on a Shoestring

I usually encourage people at conferences to do two things the next morning simply because they are easy and free: (1) Create a Google alert for their brand name, and (2) subscribe to the keyword of their brand name via YouTube. This can overwhelm the inbox, but it is free. Social-media monitoring can cost hundreds or thousands of dollars per month.

There are a number of social-media monitoring tools and services identified by J. D. Beebe in "The New Anti-Social: Free Ways to Track and Trend Online (and a Few Ways to Pay, too)." Some of these tools allow individuals to track trending words, and some allow companies to track specific words or terms. Some also provide crude sentiment ratings (the tone of terms in social media that surround the brand or company's name). Some even allow a company to compare its social-media presence with that of a competitor.

An agency would typically use a service like Radian6, Visible Measures, or Nielsen Buzzmetric, and want analysis and recommendations. But that's not typically a wise investment for a small entity.

Here are a few free tools that can help people monitor what is being written about their cause or company.

- **Trendrr.com.** Easily create new tracking trends on a myriad of platforms. Easily track trends of Facebook application use, Craigslist jobs, last.fm stats, Google news, Amazon/eBay products, Google search results, Twitter results, Fickr and FriendFeed stats, Facebook event tracking, tons of video sites tracking, and some compete.com analysis.

- **www.google.com/trends.** Use keywords to track Google Search queries throughout time, check stories on a timeline, and see geographically where the buzz is coming from.

- **http://blogpulse.com/trend.** BlogPulse Trend Search allows you to create graphs that visually track the buzz over time for certain keywords, phrases, or links. Compare search terms and links in isolation, or use all three fields to compare search terms and links against others.

- **http://technorati.com/chart/.** Technorati Tracking charts allow you to visualize the impact an individual tag or term has via a graph on its frequency across the Web.

Video Distribution Services

There are some small businesses that, for a reasonable fee, can produce and distribute video content to a variety of sites. As long as the cost is minimal (a few hundred dollars), it seems like money well spent. If nothing else, this increases the chance a small business can be optimized on search engines. I would urge entrepreneurs to be very specific about what words to target (via keywords and tagging), and to ensure the video is informative and entertaining.

If I were trying to market my own jewelry, for instance, I would likely make this investment (but not in lieu of sending free samples to popular YouTube webstars).

Before you pay a distribution service, be sure to ask about what performance you can realistically expect. It's fairly easy to manipulate "views" and give people a false sense of accomplishment. Ask a distribution service for several examples of how it has helped drive "quality views" (those that reach the right audience and drive behavior).

Power of How-To

As we reviewed in the context of search engines, two terms are increasingly being used in searches: *how to* and *video*. Entrepreneurs, whether providing a service or product, would do well to create how-to videos that answer questions their prospects may ask. For instance, if I sold a device that helped people catch or kill moles that devastate healthy lawns, I would post an instructional video that educated viewers on the variety of methods to use. The video would be primarily educational, but indicate some of the limitations of alternative solutions and correct many of the myths. At the end, I'd gently introduce my product and provide a link to my online store.

An individual is likely to approach Google with a search like "how to get rid of moles," and find a variety of articles or advertisements pertaining to the subject. But it's likely that Google would eventually provide a top ranking to a helpful video that educated the searcher—especially if the average viewer watched at least 30 to 90 seconds.

CHAPTER 16

Learning from Obama Girl

By Ben Relles, founder of BarelyPolitical.com

In this chapter you will learn:

- What one of the most viral sensations of the decade, Obama Girl, can teach you about creating and promoting your videos.

- How to take your video from online buzz to mainstream news and conversations.

- Three proven elements to online-video success based on hands-on experience with entertainment and brand case studies.

- How to adapt to the medium as it matures, and use online video to build on existing conversations.

Getting Online Video into the Mainstream Conversation

In previous chapters of this book Kevin examines how online videos are discovered most often via ways that don't fit the usual definition of viral sharing. Indeed, most often videos are discovered through search engines, subscribing to YouTube channels, or through "related videos" to the video they are watching. Kevin declared the era of *viral* video dead in 2008.

However, Kevin asked me to write this chapter in part to theorize about videos that do actually *go viral* and become part of pop culture. I created an online-video comedy network called Barely Political, which is approaching more than a half billion views. As Kevin has laid out in the book, the majority of our viewership comes through continuously building an audience—which is more sustainable than trying to "go viral" with every video.

One aspect of online video that fascinates me is that sometimes videos do indeed go viral and beyond. They begin as online videos, but develop into stories often much bigger than the original video itself. Eventually these iconic videos become fodder for television networks, "watercooler conversations," and pop culture. Within weeks the video can become significant enough of a story that Katie Couric is reporting on it, and people are discussing it not just on social media but in person. For show creators, as well as brands, this can be more valuable than views alone.

My Man Crush on Obama

The first online video I posted was called "My Box in a Box." It was perhaps even more juvenile than the majority of Kevin's videos. Two days after posting the video, a parody of a popular *Saturday Night Live* video, it was on MSNBC being named "The Viralest Video," and eventually the video was featured in *Rolling Stone* and on MTV.

The video didn't make much money—some money came in on iTunes sales and by selling the box itself (which sold on eBay for $1,500 in a charity auction).

But as someone with a marketing background, I did find the concept exciting—that with online video (and YouTube), a video could be created for several hundred dollars and be seen by millions of people—online and offline—in a matter of days.

The next video I created online was a music parody called "I Got a Crush on Obama." My goal was to create a political comedy web site, and I wanted to start with a big launch video. While I was in fact a supporter of Obama, my primary motivation was to see how many people I could reach on my second attempt at a viral video.

We tapped a perfect storm with good timing, a catchy song, and a convincing performance by our "Obama Girl" Amber Ettinger. The news media is hungry for election-related stories prior to any primaries, and "Obama Girl" quickly became a symbol of viral videos during the 2008 election. Amber appeared on *Saturday Night Live*, and just about every television news network in the United States and abroad. We were approached by three different presidential campaigns trying to persuade Obama Girl to "jump ship" to them.

Eventually the *Washington Post* and *Newsweek* both named it one of the decade's 10 most-recognized "memes" (Internet phenomenon). Though I think the term "viral" is often a misnomer, Obama Girl did rely on "viral" sharing, and served as an ideal launching pad for our network.

The online-video networks I now oversee as part of Next New Networks—Barely Political and Barely Digital—are definitely examples of the principles Kevin has outlined in this book. The vast majority of the more than 450 million views we've had since launching come from our subscribers, e-mail lists, and search-engine inquiries.

Three Tips for Infusing Online Video into Culture

Since Kevin has covered video strategies and tactics broadly, I will summarize three specific things I believe have the most impact on a video going "beyond viral video" and into pop culture and mainstream media.

Be Really Quick

A lot of marketing agencies espouse the importance of being "conversational," and creating ideas so compelling that they initiate conversations. I have found it is often easier to join a conversation already taking place with online video rather than start a new one.

We shot the Obama Girl video on a Friday and posted within a week. The video benefited from several major trends, including the suddenly rising candidacy of Barack Obama and the unprecedented impact of YouTube on that election.

But online video indisputably benefits from speed. We once created an Ann Coulter video after she proclaimed on TV that "Jews Need to Be Perfected." However by the time we posted our video, the story was no longer news.

I believe brands that are able to act quickly—whether with their own videos or partnering with popular video creators—have a unique opportunity to do something interesting and be part of the conversation.

Obama himself knew this. Two days after the Reverend Wright story became big, he addressed the issue. The

37-minute video of his speech was seen 20 million times online. And it was credited with deflecting a potentially major problem.

To accomplish the necessary speed, it's important to follow an audience's conversation. This is best accomplished by having someone dedicated to monitoring the conversations. Using tools like summize.com, Yahoo! Buzz, and Google Trends, brands and studios can know what their audience is talking about at any moment. Most important, brands and entertainers need a plan in place to capitalize on a situation so they can react quickly to news about which their audiences care.

Be Really Different

While riskier than partnering with established networks, brands have created their own "viral" phenomena just by being so remarkably unique that people are compelled to share their video. A video, generally speaking, becomes viral when more people are compelled to stop and send it to other people—rather than moving on to whatever else they were doing. Have a video that one in ten people share? It will fizzle in a few days. Have a video that two in three people share? The views will accumulate quickly.

Sometimes it's luck of the draw for brands. I agree with Kevin's premise that working with online creators and studios with a track record is a better bet than chasing a "big idea." Sometimes viral video—the kind Kevin says died in 2008—can work and the benefits can outweigh "integration" or "most mentions."

Next New Networks partnered with the Gregory Brothers, a group of Brooklyn-based musicians, to build "Auto Tune the News." I had nothing to do with creating these videos, but they do happen to be my favorite online-video series in recent history. I would attribute their success to being completely unique and original—a refreshing departure from what we've seen online or on television. The Gregory Brothers have since collaborated with T-Pain, appeared on MTV and CBS, and worked with brands including Sony and Warner Brothers.

Mythology: Have a Story Behind the Video

The goal with online video should be to improve the opinion your audience has of your brand or entertainment platform. Even better, we hope to change their behavior.

One way to "stand out" is to make your video a bigger story than the video itself. A video being seen 2 million times on YouTube is no longer newsworthy itself, as thousands of videos have done that. However, some of the online videos that do end up in mainstream media do so because the story of the videos' creation is more interesting than the videos themselves.

From the beginning of online video, that was the case. Some videos were able to move beyond online video blogs because the story was fascinating. LonelyGirl15—a scripted but interactive web series that received significant media attention in 2006 and 2007—was fantastic storytelling. Even five years later, it may be the most innovative use of online video I have seen. What made the series popular was the intense debate about whether the videos were real or performance.

Brands have accomplished this as well. Samsung ended up on the news not only because it got 600 sheep to spell "Samsung." The mystery behind the story was equally compelling . . . "Wait, how exactly did they pull that off?"

Justin Bieber launched a career doing cover songs in his living room in Ontario, Canada. The story is not the videos themselves or his tens of millions of views. The story is that Justin Bieber took an unlikely road to fame, and was signed to a label and singing with Usher.

The Obama Girl series followed a similar pattern. At first, people cared about the videos. Eventually, most of our coverage came from issues like who Obama Girl was voting for.

The mythology behind a video is a key ingredient to its success. A great story behind a good video can trump a great video standing alone.

Often, the mainstream media can be a powerful way to drive online viewership as they seek ways to cover this emerging media. Mainstream media is evolving, but still very relevant and very influential.

No Secret Formula

While these are three elements that can make a video gain traction and propel it into pop culture, there are really no hard-and-fast rules to online-video success.

In some cases, creators can start a video with the intent of building an online audience, but end up with something different: They can reach exponentially more people than a YouTube video because they become part of the national conversation. Like you, I have seen terrible videos viewed several million times, and brilliant ones that are mostly undiscovered. I have seen "authentic" video creators detailing their lives in front of huge audiences, and completely "inauthentic" video creators amass millions of viewers and followers with scripted content.

There is no question that online videos can be effective in building brands. Their effect is real and can be measured. These three elements certainly can increase the likelihood of achieving success.

But much like Academy Award–winning movies, best-selling novels, and Broadway hits, there is no single formula that will produce a surefire success every time. The best we can do is keep refining our approach in an ever-changing social, cultural, and technological environment.

Generally speaking, I advise any individual creator or brand to consider ways of building their continuing audience, because that is the key to online viewership. That said, in some cases, unique and shareable video with an interesting story behind it is the best way to start building a loyal and returning audience.

As the founder and creative director of Barely Political, **Ben Relles** has established himself as a leader in digital entertainment. The comedy network launched in 2007 with Ben's video "I Got a Crush on Obama," which quickly became one of the most talked-about online videos of all time. Barely Political was later acquired by Next New Networks. Videos on Ben's comedy networks have been viewed over 450 million times and featured in media including MTV, ABC, NBC, and *Rolling Stone*. Prior to starting Barely Political, Ben received his MBA from the Wharton School of Business and spent time working on marketing strategies for brands including Nissan, Pepsi, and Snickers. He currently lives with his wife and two children outside of Philadelphia.

CHAPTER 17

Insider Information

Behind the Curtain

In this chapter you will learn:

- Who some of the top video creators are, and what they have learned to build and sustain popularity.

- Tips from two other authors of online video (Steve Garfield and Alan Lastufka) based on their own experience as video creators.

- How these webstars have turned hobbies into full-time professions that have given brands unsurpassed access to consumers online.

As online video matures, we will eventually see a television-like business model that substantiates teams of specialists—from writers and actors to directors and producers. In its infancy, however, online video has rewarded not the rock stars or one-hit wonders but the "one-man bands." These are individuals who can often act, write, edit, produce, animate, score music, and produce. They're often their own agents, and most may lack marketing degrees or experience... but they're marketers in my book.

These "amateurs" have insider information on what works in online video, and they can teach us more than any author, agency, or consultant. The medium is so rapidly evolving that there is a profound knowledge belonging to those who make a full-time living creating videos, watching them, and interacting with fans and fellow webstars. When I take even a few weeks away from YouTube, it's like returning to any other occupation after being away for years.

In this chapter, we turn back the curtain of YouTube to meet some people you may not know and whose videos you may or may not like. But they've proven their ability to crack the code and evolve with the maturing marketplace, adjusting their style as the marketplace matures.

Some of the leading webstars, authors, and video pioneers provide some insights that can help even the most accomplished brands, producers, or entrepreneurs. I asked them—via in-person and virtual interviews—to share their profiles, what keeps them persisting, and what advice they have for companies and causes.

Rhett and Link

Rhett and Link are a North Carolina–based comedy duo consisting of lifelong best friends, Rhett McLaughlin and Link Neal. The self-proclaimed "Internetainers" are best known for their musical comedy and crazy local commercials. Since 2007, Rhett and Link have been making a living almost exclusively from brand integration with their Web videos.

Rhett and Link spent the summer of 2008 releasing videos for the Alka-Seltzer Great American Road Trip. The series won the Gold award in the Consumer Goods category at *Advertising Age*'s 2008 W3 Awards, as well as best online campaign at *Adweek*'s 2008 Buzz Awards. The series also picked up two Golds (Best Campaign, Best Single) and a Craft award (Music) at the 2009 Bessies, and received two golds in the interactive category for Viral Marketing and Business to Consumer Web Site at the 2009 Advertising & Design Club of Canada Awards

Rhett McLaughlin and Link Neal, a musical comedy duo, have produced dozens of sponsored videos for leading brands.

www.RhettandLink.com
www.youtube.com/RhettandLink

What got you started, and what's kept you going?

Initially, we simply saw the Internet as a way to showcase our work. Our small, initial success led to a big opportunity to host a network television show. We thought, "That was easy." Then the show got canned after four episodes. Our backs were against the wall, so we determined to make a living through our videos and began to approach potential sponsors. That model has slowly turned into sponsors approaching us. We are now in a steady cycle of considering new clients and executing new projects.

What's ahead for you? Are you adjusting your focus given the changes in online video?

We were making a living through brand integration before we were ever making any revenue from ads associated with our content (such as the overlays and banners for YouTube Partner channels). As a result, our typical workflow is very reactive. We are approached by a brand or agency that has a product to sell or brand message to broadcast. We then custom-build a campaign or single video. We're moving towards doing more proactive content, where we have ideas for videos or series that we know will please our fan base, then we incorporate appropriate brands into those concepts.

What tips do you have for companies that wish to market their products and services via this medium?

Companies must do more than simply assess how well a brand message was disseminated, or what the customer response was to a certain product campaign. They must also consider how their brand is perceived in the process. Sure, you may be able to move a healthy number of products by dropping a 30-second pre-roll into videos, but you'll be "that brand that annoyed me when I was trying to watch the video I wanted to watch." Brands that respect the dynamics of the social Web are investing in their future, and that will lead to effecting messaging and sales.

What has been the most interesting moment(s) of your rise to fame? When did it become real, or what

is one of the more fascinating parts of your experience?

We had a bit of premature fame when we hosted the TV show. Because of that, our profile was higher than it should have been based on our content. It's been a very steady build since then. We don't have that one video that we can point to that did it for us. We always ask fans how they found us, and it's always a different video. The most interesting aspect of Internet fame is the irony of being recognized on the streets of major cities around the United States, but your neighbor having absolutely no idea what you do for a living.

What advice do you have for fellow creators?

Don't be afraid of brands. Advertising has driven entertainment for a long time. Brands can actually make your content better and your audience happier if you do it right.

From your perspective, what companies have really cracked online video well?

Microbilt sponsored our "I Love Local Commercials" series, and has been a great client. They were willing to try something new and listen to us as the Web insiders. The project is still ongoing as we write this, but it's shaping up to be a wonderful success (Taco Bell Fast Food Folk Song: www.youtube.com/watch?v=-uwY3sjqYX0).

Jodie Rivera

Jodie Rivera, a 25-year-old actress and singer, maintains a one-woman channel as the "VenetianPrincess," and is the

Jodie is the most-subscribed female musicians on YouTube, and her song parodies have led to sponsored promotions with such brands as Kellogg's Pop-Tarts.

Photo credit: Hector Rivera
www.youtube.com/venetian princess
www.vprincess.com

number one most-subscribed female musician of all time. She studied opera as a coloratura soprano at the New England Conservatory of Music in Boston, and her "7 Things Guys Don't Have to Do" music video was named as one of the most viral by *PC World* magazine.

What got you started, and what's kept you going?

I've always been involved in film and theater. YouTube was a way for me to do my own mini-shows and have complete creative freedom and control. It has become my job, and I am very grateful for that. I am my own boss, and I do what I love. That is enough to keep me going for as long as my audience will keep watching.

What's ahead for you? Are you adjusting your focus given the changes in online video?

I have a lot of brand-integration projects in the short-term future. I also have several traditional media offers on the table that I am trying to explore and figure out what would be a good route for me.

What tips do you have for companies that wish to market their products and services via this medium?

I would recommend that they go straight to successful online video creators. People who have built audiences themselves know what works and what doesn't as far as marketing in the online-video world. In-your-face ads don't seem to be as successful as organic brand integration, where the video creator is given freedom to strategically place the product in the video to seem less commercial and more real.

What has been the most interesting moment(s) of your rise to fame?

My most interesting moments have been meeting my viewers in person. The majority of my demographic is made up of teen girls, and so almost every time I go to the mall they stop me. I'm actually a shy person, but these experiences have helped me to come out of my shell. It's amazing to meet these people, who in reality are strangers to me—but they know me well. It's interesting to meet the people who have essentially brought me where I am today.

When did it become real, or what is one of the more fascinating parts of your experience?

I think it became real when I started getting press internationally. People were sending me magazines with articles about me from Israel, Vietnam, France, Rome, and so on. It's fascinating to think that I am known all around the world. At times, it's hard to fathom.

What advice to you have for fellow creators?

I tell them to find their niche. If you look at the most-subscribed list, everybody has their thing that they are known for. I do celebrity parodies, and others do comedic sketches. Before I found spoof music videos, I experimented with different types of videos. Sometimes you need to do that to find what sticks. Topical videos tend to do well.

From your perspective, what companies have really cracked online video well?

I think corporate channels like The Onion and College Humor have really cracked online video well. They produce good-quality content that has viral integrity.

Greg Benson

Greg Benson has created or directed numerous comedy viral video hits and web series, including "Gorgeous Tiny Chicken Machine Show" (distributed by Sony), "Retarded Policeman" (viewed over 50 million times at YouTube), and "The Guild" (Best Series winner in the Yahoo!, YouTube, and Streamy awards, and distributed by Microsoft). Greg's short films and prank videos have also had millions of online views, and have integrated brands such as Pizza Hut, Polk Audio, AT&T, and MTV. MediocreFilms is one of

Greg Benson, a Los Angeles actor, director, and producer, has created a number of wildly popular Web series.

www.mediocrefilms.com
http://youtube.com/mediocrefilms
http://twitter.com/mediocrefilms

the all-time top-subscribed channels on YouTube, and Greg's projects have had over 100 million views Web-wide.

What got you started, and what's kept you going?

I've been working as a professional actor in Los Angeles since 1991 and have been shooting my own comedy sketches since 1992. In the 1990s, the only outlet for my videos was public access TV. But once online video emerged around 2005, I began to share my videos on my own web site. In 2006, my brilliant wife (Web producer Kim Evey) convinced me to join the MySpace and YouTube communities, and once I saw the power of social networking, it pushed me forward to create more content. My first video featured on YouTube was "Greg Hits Hollywood," which got nearly a million views and brought me my first several thousand subscribers. The reward of having my work seen by more people than I could possibly reach in any other medium available to me is what kept me going. YouTube has also opened doors for Kim and me to pitch and sell successful web series to companies like Sony and Microsoft.

What's ahead for you? Are you adjusting your focus given the changes in online video?

For many popular video makers like myself, YouTube has become a full-time job. I recognize the value of creating quality content on a regular basis, and have greatly increased the frequency of my uploads to retain a loyal fan base. I also make sure my branded videos and product placement videos are always entertaining, so that even if viewers realize the video revolves around a product they will still enjoy themselves and, hopefully, pass it on.

What tips do you have for companies that wish to market their products and services via this medium?

Hopefully, advertisers [will be] smart enough to recognize what makes one of my videos popular and enjoyable, and not try to shift that too much with their own product's message. There is a way of fitting products within videos naturally so that it doesn't interfere with the humor of a video, and doesn't hit the viewer over the head with a sales message. If viewers feel they are only watching an advertisement, it could turn them away.

What has been the most interesting moment(s) of your rise to fame? When did it become real, or what is one of the more fascinating parts of your experience?

After MySpace and YouTube featured another one of my videos (my wife Kim Evey's pilot for "Gorgeous Tiny Chicken Machine Show," which I directed), the e-mails and calls started coming in from studios and online companies that wanted to meet with us. Suddenly it seemed everyone was interested in this show and hearing pitches from us for other shows. The process of pitching wasn't new to us (we had both pitched TV projects), so we had fun and our meetings led to several deals. That was the shift from making videos for fun on our own time to having delivery schedules for 10-episode seasons, and budgets to increase the quality of our work. We also began to employ cast and crew (paying back the people who had previously worked for us for free), bought high-end equipment, and so on. Before we knew it, video production had changed from a hobby to a full-time job! Around this time, the YouTube Partner Program also launched, so all of our videos there were earning revenue. And my videos were also featured on numerous TV shows such as *The Maury Povich Show* (which hired me to shoot a new "Greg Hits Hollywood 2") and *Good Morning America* (which picked "Greg Hits Hollywood" as one of the Top 5 Viral Videos of the Year).

What advice to you have for fellow creators?

The main tip I give is to keep shooting, editing, and uploading on a regular basis. The more work you put into it, the better the results will be in the quality of your videos and (hopefully) the number of viewers. Don't underestimate the power of social networking; keeping in touch with fans helps them feel involved and gives them a personal connection to you. For writers, I stress the importance of writing what you know—don't try to cater to what you think your audience might like, but do what amuses you. For would-be filmmakers, I recommend the cheapest, best film school around: DVD director commentaries and behind-the-scenes videos. And the bottom line is, the more time you spend on YouTube, the more you'll get out of it. Look at what other people are doing and you'll get to know the tricks that might help new viewers find you.

From your perspective, what companies have really cracked online video well?

I've seen some extremely clever viral campaigns that have done a great job for brand recognition, like Ray-Ban ("Guy catches glasses with face") and the multichannel Carl's Jr. campaign. I've also seen some fail dramatically by trying to fake a viral video poorly, like the downright awful Coors "Perfect Pour" videos.

Steve Garfield

Steve Garfield is a videographer and video blogger based in Boston. One of the Internet's first video bloggers, Garfield began experimenting with the technique in 2002 and launched his own video blog on January 1, 2004. He is the author of *Get Seen: Online Video Secrets to Building Your Business*, and was inducted into the International Academy of Web Television in 2009.

Steve Garfield has written a book about online video, and was one of the most prominent early video bloggers years before YouTube launched.

What got you started, and what's kept you going?

I got started putting video on the Web on January 1, 2004, as a technical experiment. I had a blog, and I was making videos, so I wanted to figure out how to add video to the blog.

It turned out that others were also experimenting with the technology and we found each other on Yahoo! Groups. The unexpected consequence of watching each other's videos was that we got to know each other. We became friends.

It became more than just putting video on the Web. We discovered in those early days that a lot more was happening. Connections were formed, and it was all because of the visual medium that we used to share moments with each other.

I like to say that "I subscribe to people." It's more to me than just one-shot videos that you watch and move on from. It's a relationship, and that's what's kept me producing and watching videos since 2004.

What's ahead for you? Are you adjusting your focus given the changes in online video?

I'm still doing the same thing that I was back in 2004, only more so. I am focused on helping people put video on the Web, and like to demystify the process. I'll write blog posts and create videos that explain, step-by-step, the process to put video online. That's why I wrote the second book in this series, *Get Seen: Online Video Secrets to Building Your Business*. In the book, I explain all the things I've been writing about on the Web for the past six years. It's all nice and organized and easy to follow.

What tips do you have for companies that wish to market their products and services via this medium?

What I do on the Web is provide knowledge, examples, and how-to content that relates to putting video on the Web. I've got a book site, http://stevegarfield.com/getseen, where I have tutorials, blog posts, and videos. There's lots of free content there, and by giving all that away, people might be interested in buying the book.

The site also serves the purpose of updating content from the book. So it's like a living extension of the book, featuring new products, sites, and how-to posts.

My site is a community for like-minded people to come and share their knowledge. It's not just me posting, but others who have read the book and want to share their progress.

What has been the most interesting moment(s) of your rise to fame? When did it become real, or what is one of the more fascinating parts of your experience?

Since my book came out, I've been extremely satisfied by reading the reader reviews. It really makes all the hard work of writing the book worthwhile to see others enjoy reading it.

What advice to you have for fellow creators?

I tell video creators to become comfortable with the video-making process. There will be moments when you want to capture video, and you don't want to be unfamiliar with your camera at that moment. It should be second nature to you: how to hold the camera, where to stand, how to get good lighting and audio.

The other thing I tell creators is to be authentic and real. I tend to shoot unscripted videos, usually interviews. It's okay to ask the interviewee to restate something if you don't think it'll come out the way you want in your final video. That's directing, and when you know what you want, it's okay to direct an interview.

The third thing I encourage creators to do is to participate in the community around your video. Don't just post it and forget it. Once you post your video, your job really starts. You've got to engage with your viewers by watching the comments and replying.

From your perspective, what companies have really cracked online video well?

BMW has done a good job of putting video on the Web that's accessible. They shoot video of car designers and have them share their knowledge. And BMW isn't afraid of letting the video go a little longer than your average Web video.

Hank Green

Hank Green has been making YouTube videos since 2006, and is most fascinated by how community has become such a vital part of entertainment. He's trying to capture this to make money and deliver products with his YouTube-specific record label DFTBA Records, which had over

Hank Green and his brother John spent a year communicating exclusively via public videos. The experiment, vlogbrothers, created a community of people known as "Nerdfighters."

www.dftba.com

www.youtube.com/vlogbrothers

$200,000 in revenues in 2009. He also works with communities to help make the world a better place, and has several projects focused on charity. He helped YouTube launch its Video Volunteers program and organizes the yearly "Project for Awesome," in which all of YouTube works together to promote charities.

What got you started, and what's kept you going?

The one and only thing that got me started was that my big brother wanted to do this with me. What's kept me going is an obligation to him, our community, and a very deep interest in the evolution of entertainment.

What's ahead for you? Are you adjusting your focus given the changes in online video?

John and I have shifted our thinking to include both show-format projects as well as conversation-format ideas. The first example of this is "Truth or Fail," an online, interactive, YouTube-based trivia game. We've got some other more thematically based ideas in the works as well, but we're never leaving the conversation format behind—ever.

What tips do you have for companies that wish to market their products and services via this medium?

You have to utilize already-successful people and projects, but you can't just drop a pile of money in people's laps and expect them to go along with you. Give content creators a reason to want to work with you. Give them opportunities, not just money. Give them (and their viewers) a reason to feel good about your company.

What has been the most interesting moment(s) of your rise to fame? When did it become real, or what is one of the more fascinating parts of your experience?

The first time I was recognized in public was a pretty big deal, but the biggest slap-in-the-face moment was when a sick young woman wanted us to be her Make-A-Wish

Foundation wish. We told her to save her wish and we just came by and hung out for a few hours. She was awesome, and her mom fried ravioli for us. Fried ravioli and hanging out, as far as I'm concerned, is way better than fame.

What advice to you have for fellow creators?

You have to be entertaining, yes. You have to give people a reason to watch one video. But, much more than that, you have to give them a reason to watch two, three, four, or fifty videos. That comes in the form of consistency and fostering community. In a world of infinite entertaining content, you have to create a relationship with your viewers. You have to create a community. And, in the end, a community is a much more exciting, useful, and fun thing to have than just a bunch of fans.

From your perspective, what companies have really cracked online video well?

Well, DFTBA Records has done a pretty good job:-). I haven't really seen too many vast successes in this space actually, so I'm going to elect not to answer.

Alan Lastufka

Alan Lastufka is the author of *YouTube: An Insider's Guide to Climbing the Charts* (O'Reilly Media) and co-owner of DFTBA Records, a record label that signs YouTube musicians exclusively. Lastufka's videos on YouTube have received over 5.5 million views and he has written and edited viral videos for such content creators as Michael Buckley (WhatTheBuckShow) and former *MADtv* cast member Lisa Donovan (LisaNova).

Alan Lasufka created a record label of YouTube musicians, wrote an insider book about YouTube, and actively partners and helps leading YouTube webstars.

http://youtube.com/fallofautu-mndistro (Alan's personal YouTube channel)
http://dftba.com (Alan's record label)

What got you started, and what's kept you going?

I stumbled upon "Ask A Ninja" while home sick from work. I clicked around YouTube and found an amazing community of talented content creators hanging out just beneath the viral videos. The YouTube editors featured a number of my early videos, and I was a Partner in no time. Using YouTube as not only a community, but also as a promotional vehicle for my music and my label has kept me on the site for hours each and every day.

What's ahead for you? Are you adjusting your focus given the changes in online video?

I'm much more behind the scenes these days. I do a lot of freelance writing, editing, and motion graphics work for other YouTube channels. I still post videos, but most are related to my business, the record label. In the last month, we were featured in a front-page article in the *Chicago Tribune*'s Red Eye Entertainment section, we were spotlighted on YouTube's official blog, and we were named "Best Online Music Label of the Year" by Mashable. So while I may not be uploading as often as I have in previous years, I'm still involved on a daily basis.

What tips do you have for companies that wish to market their products and services via this medium?

Don't try to trick anyone. People will be able to see through it. If you're doing product placement, be obvious and cheeky about it, or do something so freakin' cool that no one will care that you paid the content creator to hold your product while doing it. Most popular video makers have a very dedicated audience who trust the host. Find a video maker who fits your brand and the views and clickthroughs will follow.

What has been the most interesting moment(s) of your rise to fame? When did it become real, or what is one of the more fascinating parts of your experience?

Hollywood film star Kevin Pollak (*Casino*, *The Usual Suspects*) contacted me after reading my YouTube book and asked if I'd consult on building his YouTube channel. We ended up making a number of videos together, the first of which was tweeted by YouTube's official Twitter account. I grew up watching Kevin's movies on television. It was pretty surreal to be editing and directing him.

What advice to you have for fellow creators?

Interact. Don't upload a video and walk away. Don't ignore your comments or video responses, or "at replies" on Twitter. You need to be connected and responsive. People always notice when I leave a comment on their video response, or reply to their comments on my videos. They don't forget that. It builds a strong and fruitful bond between viewer and creator.

From your perspective, what companies have really cracked online video well?

Ford perfected online-video promotion with their Fiesta project. Ford gave a couple dozen select YouTubers free cars and free gas for six months, then sent them on missions which they were to record and upload to their YouTube channels. It was interactive, transparent, and entertaining.

Charles Trippy

Charles Trippy, one of YouTube's most-viewed creators is a 25-year-old who, along with his fiancée, Alli Speed, is documenting each day in video format and sharing these videos online. Their project, "Internet Killed Television"

Charles Trippy recently spent a year posting his own daily home-made reality show called "Internet Killed Television."

www.youtube.com/Charles
www.youtube.com/charlestrippy
www.InternetKilledTelevision.com

is a Web-based series (or homemade reality show) that won Mashable's Third Annual Web Awards. Trippy appeared as a contestant on *Who Wants to Be an Internet Millionare* and in the HBO Labs series *Hooking Up*.

What got you started, and what's kept you going?

Started? Just loved to goof around with a camera with my friends. Going? The viewers. It's amazing reading feedback from all over the world (good and bad).

What's ahead for you? Are you adjusting your focus given the changes in online video?

I've been fortunate enough to be able to do this for the last 5 years—hopefully, I'll be able to adjust and keep doing it another 5 or 10!:)

What tips do you have for companies that wish to market their products and services via this medium?

Going viral is really just random. It's hard to generate a formula that works each time—it keeps changing. The best bet is to stay edgy!

What has been the most interesting moment(s) of your rise to fame? When did it become real, or what is one of the more fascinating parts of your experience?

Meeting Hunter Burgan and winning the Shorty Award for comedy, [and] Winning Video of the Year and Brand of the Year has been really amazing. Being able to share my and my fiancée's daily life on the Internet has been really awesome, too!

What advice to you have for fellow creators?

I say to make whatever makes you laugh. You have to be happy with what you make at the end of the day.

From your perspective, what companies have really cracked online video well?

I think Axe is doing pretty well. Other than that I don't really know—it seems that every company has at least one good online video, but that doesn't mean they are always good!

Dane Boedigheimer

Dane Boedigheimer is known as "DaneBoe," and is a freelance film-maker who produces videos for the Web. He runs a comedy video web site, gagfilms.com, and creates the major-ity of content on it. His series, "Annoying Orange," became an online meme (Web phe-nomenon) in early 2010, in one month surpassing the views of television's most-watched show (Fox's *American Idol*). His videos have been viewed more than 150 million times and have been featured on televi-sion and many popular

Dane Boedigheimer was already a hit with GagFilms, but has gener-ated unprecedented success with his talking fruits in "Annoying Orange."

http://youtube.com/daneboe
http://annoyingorange.com

video-sharing sites such as YouTube, Yahoo!, Dailymotion, StupidVideos, MSN, Crackle, Break, Metacafe, Aniboom, Revver, Spike, and JibJab.

What got you started, and what's kept you going?

I've been making videos since I was 13 when my parents pur-chased an eight-millimeter camcorder. I have always been fascinated with creating videos with fantastical elements (talking food, time travel, aliens, etc.). I love taking our world and integrating it with fantasy and sci-fi elements. I love making people laugh. Nothing makes me happier than getting e-mails from people letting me know how much they and their family/friends love my videos and quote lines from them. I grew up quoting movies, so to know that people are out there quoting my videos blows my mind. It's a dream come true. What keeps me going is the love of creating and making people laugh.

What's ahead for you? Are you adjusting your focus given the changes in online video?

I am concentrating more on the Annoying Orange episodes. So far the series has proven extremely successful and I want to continue trying to increase its success not only on the Web, but also transitioning to other mediums like television or film. I would also love to create a feature-length film at some point, but I am extremely happy working in "short form" the way I am now. It allows a lot of freedom to be as creative as I want. Honestly, I hope to change and grow as online video evolves, so that I can continue to keep doing what I'm doing!

What's ahead for you? Are you adjusting your focus given the changes in online video?

I completely agree with your statement—we have to remember that the Internet is pretty unpredictable. You can make the greatest video you've ever made and it might flop when you release it. The key is to do what other people have done well—but do it better! Make your video stand out. Stay edgy. Put a spin on an old idea. No one wants to watch a guy in a suit talking to the camera . . . but a talking orange? Internet gold.

What has been the most interesting moment(s) of your rise to fame? When did it become real, or what is one of the more fascinating parts of your experience?

By far my most interesting moments have been creating the Annoying Orange character. To watch something that I created become bigger than me is astounding. For example, Annoying Orange has 10 times more followers on Twitter than me. And on Facebook my 18,000 followers pale in comparison to nearly a million following Annoying Orange.

I now have managers and a lawyer to help expand the Annoying Orange brand and hopefully take it to new levels. People have contacted me about making Annoying Orange toys, iPhone applications, advertisements, and other extensions. It is an awesome thing to create a character that takes on a life of its own and becomes bigger than you. It's also a little weird. But hey, I can't complain.

What advice to you have for fellow creators?

I get questions all the time about how I do my special effects, how YouTube works, how to get popular on YouTube, as well as camera and editing tips. I just tell people to practice, practice, practice! It's the only way you learn. I help give tips, but I can only help so much. Much of learning the ins and outs of online video comes from failing and succeeding on your own—figuring out what works for you.

From your perspective, what companies have really cracked online video well?

Machinima.com has done really well. The web site's owners pay numerous online video creators to make videos, which helps get creators additional exposure in the process. They give creators complete creative control over what they want to produce for them, and are smart about cross-promotion. They are the seventh most-subscribed channel on YouTube for good reason.

Shay Butler

Shay Butler, 30, is deeply religious and identifies first as a husband and father. The former "blue collar" worker was a radio personality in Idaho when he launched his quickly popular "ShayCarl" and "Shaytards" YouTube channels, where they have more than 1 billion subscribers. Shay and his wife Katilette and their four children moved temporarily to Venice Beach, California, to take on daily video blogging. He currently commutes between Idaho and California, where he participates as part of a YouTube collaboration network called "The Station."

What got you started, and what's kept you going?

I was 27 years old, married with three kids, and I was almost hitting a midlife crisis. I was thinking to myself, "Is this it?"

Shay Butler turned his radio gig into a vibrant online-video career, and climbed the most subscribed charts faster than almost anyone to date.

http://youtube.com/shaycarl
www.youtube.com/shaytards

and "Is this my life?" I had a granite job and was a disk jockey. But one day I saw Philip DeFranco (Sxephil) on YouTube, and thought . . . I think I can do that!

What's ahead for you? Are you adjusting your focus given the changes in online video?

I don't know what's ahead. In order to stay relevant it seems like you always have to evolve or reinvent yourself in some way. I've always done things like growing my beard out to a ridiculous length. So it seems like I've always created these events that get people wanting to see what happens.

You can't stay stagnant with videos. There has to be something to look forward to. Our next big event is having another baby.

I'm creating web sites, selling t-shirts, and people are trying to make television shows from my video. I really don't know what's going to happen, or what I want to happen. I am not sure I want to be a big movie star and famous.

What has been the most interesting moment(s) of your rise to fame? When did it become real, or what is one of the more fascinating parts of your experience?

It still doesn't seem real. To me, it's going to end in two weeks. I've got two weeks for this whole YouTube thing to continue. I guess the first time I got my first check from YouTube it was $350, and I was like, "Holy crap . . . they're paying me to have fun on camera."

The real answer is I still don't feel it's real. In the back of my mind it feels like this is going to end any day now. And I'm going to go back to polishing granite.

I want it to continue because I love it, but it honestly seems too good to be true. Oh, that reminds me of some cliché from an Oscar speech, but I hear stats about 98 percent of people hating their jobs . . . and I feel like I'm one of the luckiest people in the world.

What advice do you have for fellow creators?

The advice I have is to *do what you like.* There are so many things you can do. Make friends with other YouTube people and network. For instance, when I joined The Station I had just hit 100,000 subscribers. Less than a year later I have more than 500,000. I've literally quadrupled my subscription base by working with other YouTubers.

From your perspective, what companies have really cracked online video well?

I think Take180 (T180 Studios, owned by Disney) knows what it's doing. On the other hand, you've got PopTub, which spent millions and only got 30,000 subscribers.

I encourage companies to listen to YouTube personalities, and allow creators to have free reign. When we did a "flash mob" video for a client it was successful because the sponsor gave us room.

CHAPTER 18
The Future of Online Video

In this chapter you will learn:

- How online-video, mobile viewing, and television are merging, and will continue to collide.

- Who will win the race for eyeballs (amateur webstars or professional content creators)?

- How marketing and advertising needs to evolve with technology and consumer preferences.

- How marketing and entertainment can coexist to provide consumers with quality content for free.

The nice thing about covering online video since 2005 on a blog is that you can selectively draw the reader's attention to what you predicted accurately, and hope nobody discovers where your crystal ball was murky.

I have predicted certain milestones with precision, but I am surprised at two things that haven't changed more drastically. First, I would have thought webstars would be passé by now. Second, I would have imagined online video and television as colliding earlier.

Lean Forward Meets Lean Back

In *Back to the Future*, Marty (played by Michael J. Fox) returns to 1955 and mentions to his grandparents that he has more than one television set. Marty's grandmother dismisses it as a joke because "nobody has two television sets." As a newlywed in 1996, I remember debating between a Dell media center or personal computer. We ultimately decided our *one* household computer needed to be at a desk where we kept bills and paperwork.

Since that time I have had four children, yet with a few exceptions television and online-video viewing remain discretely different tasks. We "lean forward" at our computers and laptops, but "lean back" to watch television shows—even if we view them "on demand."

Despite online video's explosive growth in recent years, the percentage of video viewing we consume via laptops and mobile devices is almost trivial next to the viewing we do on the couch or in bed.

Since 2007 I have been anticipating the device that would allow me to watch YouTube and Hulu from the comfort of a television, but this remains rare and complex. The vast amount of Americans do not resemble our household, which is a tangled web of countless computers, wireless mobile devices, at least four wireless networks, two cable television devices, two Ethernet-ready HDTVs, a digital-video recorder, a TiVo, an Apple TV, a Hulu, a Web-enabled Blue-ray DVD player, a Roku, and a computer media center (how quaint this picture will be when I have teenagers). I also have an annoying habit of rescuing television sets—abandoned on curbs when replaced by high-definition monitors—as if they are stray animals.

Consumer demand, while strong and growing, has not yet compelled significant change in the way cable companies operate. While many of my YouTube friends have long been without cable television, most families don't buy devices or use the Ethernet functionality on their televisions.

In years ahead, I believe that television viewing will migrate increasingly to an "on demand" model where the term "online video" will become obsolete. We'll all have preferences between the three primary screens (television, computer, mobile devices), and certain content will do better on certain forms.

Having been an annual "Chicken Little" predicting the collision of online video and television, I will say only that it will happen. When it happens is subject to market forces, where industries will defend status quo until consumer demand permits it no longer.

Professional Content Grows Faster than Webstars

In recent years, professionally produced content has begun to dominate online video viewing—YouTube and Hulu have persuaded producers and networks of the benefits to distributing content via online video. More important, the "platforms" like YouTube and Hulu have provided revenue sharing and control to content creators.

Surprisingly, webstars have continued to grow exponentially, even while professional content (music videos especially) is increasingly the "most viewed" on many web sites.

The percentage of overall video consumption online versus television remains almost trivial. This is changing, of course, and will accelerate with industry and technology evolution. The increasing online-video audience has allowed both professional creators and webstars to grow audiences.

YouTube's "most popular" and "most subscribed" videos today are mostly created by individuals rather than production studios. I do expect that to change in time. The early adopters of online video want something that television can't provide, and they prefer short-form content. As technology allows broader demographics to stream video content "on demand," we'll see consumers expecting better production quality and permitting longer forms of video.

Just as the music industry has a narrow bell curve, a small portion of producers will dominate the majority of viewing. However the "long tail" will continue to be long, and niche programming is here to stay.

Advertisers Shift from Interruption to Entertainment

There will be continued pressure on marketers to create video promotion that first educates or entertains, and gently advertises as a secondary objective. As long as viewers have active control of their experience, the 30- to 60-second advertisement will have diminished impact. Furthermore, it will irritate consumers if it delays their access to desired content.

A product pitch is annoying on television, but we perversely accept it when we're subscribed to the content. Anyone who has clutched a remote and enjoyed "on demand" video (DVR or time-shifted) can tell you the future . . . given the option, they'd opt out of even the most endearing ads.

When consumers are hunched over a computer or wielding a mobile device, their appetite for an irrelevant ad is further diminished. Advertisements—such as pre-rolls that delay a viewer's access to desired video content—may be tolerated and marginally improve awareness. However, the brand has become a conscious or unconscious irritant to the consumer, and we might agree that won't drive sustainable sales.

Alternatively, consider the audience reaction when their favorite show bakes in a "thanks to our sponsor" message in the middle of their show. Now the brand is the hero, and is enabling a viewer's experience and keeping the show's creator viable.

We won't soon pay for the majority of our video content, so most of us will tolerate it being subsidized by advertisers. My hope and expectation is that the advertising industry will evolve to meet the needs and preferences of consumers.

Madison and Hollywood Become BFFs

Media creators are dependent on advertising, and advertisers need creative content to earn audience attention. However, the vast majority of media spending in the past decade has kept marketers and entertainers intermediated by agencies, media buyers, networks, and lawyers.

Online video is enabling—and requiring in some cases—marketers and entertainers to work more closely than they are accustomed. They're not quite BFFs (best friends forever), but that day may come.

While the blurring between entertainment and promotion is not always healthy, it's also not new (it was common in the early days of radio and television). I hope marketers will partner with media buyers to go beyond online advertising in the forms of ineffective banner ads that are ultimately ignored. A brand takes on a different life when it is integrated into an engaging experience instead of interrupting it with a pre-roll or dancing for attention on the sidelines.

The Next Big Thing

I reserve the right to be completely wrong about these predictions. Had I had money to invest in 2005, I would have bet it all on Revver, which is now virtually deceased. And somewhere hiding in YouTube is a video of me urging YouTube's founders, Chad Hurley, Steven Chen, and Sequoia to sell at any price to anyone before the online-video bubble burst. I recall burning a dollar bill to make my point.

While I may not be a savvy investor, I do know that any new industry is subject to accelerated growth and gluts. Follow the money and you'll predict the changes ahead better than most.

Like the media that preceded it—stage, radio, television, and film—online video will mature. Predominant players, not amateurs and pranksters, will secure their place in the emerging marketplace. Some stars will remain relevant, and new stars will emerge.

I can make one prediction with 100 percent accuracy. As soon as we can call online video a mature marketplace, I will find it far less interesting. Fortunately, that day seems far ahead of us.

Notes

For easier access to these links, visit www.beyondviralvideo
.com and use the keywords in bold.

Introduction

1. "The Numa Story: Interview with Gary Brolsma," www
   .newnuma.com/story.html. **NUMA**
2. Mark Hendrickson, "Another Take on Getting Videos
   to Go Viral," TechCrunch.com, January 4, 2008, www
   .techcrunch.com/2008/01/04/another-take-on-getting-
   videos-to-go-viral/. **HENDRICKSON**
3. Dan Seitz, "The 7 Ballsiest Ways Anyone Has Ever
   Quit Their Job," in Cracked.com's *Weird World*,
   January 6, 2010, www.cracked.com/article/18362_the-7-
   ballsiest-ways-anyone-ever-quit-their-job/. **CRACKED**

Chapter 1

1. Tim Arango, "NBC's Slide to Troubled Nightly
   Punch," *New York Times*, January 16, 2010, www
   .nytimes.com/2010/01/17/business/media/17nbc.html?
   pagewanted=1&src=twt&twt=nytimes. **NBC**
2. Ashkan Karbasfrooshan, "Context Is King: How Videos
   Are Found and Consumed Online," TechCrunch, January 30, 2010, http://techcrunch.com/2010/01/30/
   context-is-king-how-videos-found/. **CONTEXT**
3. "Factors Behind eMarketer's Revised Online Ad
   Forecast," October 19, 2009, www.emarketer.com/
   Article.aspx?R=1007337. **FORECAST**

4. ComScore, "U.S. Online Video Market Continues Ascent as Americans Watch 33 Billion Videos in December," December 2009, http://comscore.com/ Press_Events/Press_Releases/2010/2/U.S._Online_Video_ Market_Continues_Ascent_as_Americans_Watch_33_ Billion_Videos_in_December. COMSCORE1

5. "ComScore: YouTube Now 24 Percent of All Google Searches," TechCrunch, December 19, 2008, www .techcrunch.com/2008/12/18/comscore-youtube-now-25-percent-of-all-google-searches/. COMSCORE2

6. "Numa Numa" (YouTube video) www.youtube.com/ watch?v=KmtzQCSh6xk. NUMANUMA

7. Nielsen "Three Screen Report," Via NielsenWire, March 2010, http://blog.nielsen.com/nielsenwire/ online_mobile/three-screen-report-q409/

8. Brian Morrisey, "How Far Will Consumers Go to See Your Content," *Adweek*, May 28, 2007, www .adweek.com/aw/esearch/article_display.jsp?vnu_ content_id=1003590901. ADWEEK

9. Wayne Friedman, "Online Ads Surpass TV Ads in Recall, Likability," MediaPost, April 22, 2010, www.mediapost .com/publications/?fa=Articles.showArticle&art_aid= 126671. MEDIAPOST

10. Abbey Klaassen, *Advertising Age*, "How to Make Effective Online Video Ads," January 2007, www .dynamiclogic.com/na/pressroom/coverage/docs/ 251997_final.pdf.

11. ComScore, "U.S. Online Video Market Sours in July as Summer Vacation Drives Pickup in Entertainment and Leisure Activities Online," August 27, 2009, www .comscore.com/Press_Events/Press_Releases/2009/ 8/U.S._Online_Video_Market_Soars_in_July_as_Summer_ Vacation_Drives_Pickup_in_Entertainment_and_Leisure_ Activities_Online. COMSCORE3

12. Metacafe Press Release, "Short Professional Online Video Clips Rival Television for Entertainment Value," July 7, 2009, http://press.metacafe.com/?p=155. METACAFE

Chapter 2

1. Kevin Nalty, "Trivia: Time Watching Television versus Online Video?" April 25, 2010, "WillVideoForFoood.com," http://willvideoforfood.com/2010/04/25/trivia-time-watching-television-versus-online-video/. WEBVIDEOTIME

Chapter 3

1. "Lazy Sunday," NBC's Saturday Night Live Digital Shorts via Hulu.com, www.hulu.com/watch/ 1397/saturday-night-live-snl-digital-short-lazy-sunday. LAZYSUNDAY
2. Kevin Nalty, "Scary Maze Game," posted June 27, 2008, www.youtube.com/watch?v=W2R9YTXJeWE. SCARY-MAZE
3. John Jantsch, "Using Viral Video in Small Business Marketing," Duct Tape Marketing, August 25, 2008, www.ducttapemarketing.com/blog/2008/08/25/using-viral-video-in-small-business-marketing/. PENNIES
4. YouTube Channel www.youtube.com/user/penny pranks/. PENNYPRANKS
5. Kevin Nalty, "Pennies for Tollbooth Guy," posted July 26, 2006, www.youtube.com/watch?v= DLW1JAVG81o.
6. Viral Video Chart, http://viralvideochart.unrulymedia .com/. VIRALCHART
7. "The AdAge Viral Video Chart," *Avertising Age*, "http:// adage.com/digital/archive?section_id=674. ADAGEVIRAL

8. Ashkan Karbasfrooshan, "Online Video Content: In Search of Benchmarks," WatchMojo.com, February 23, 2009, http://watchmojo.com/blog/business/2009/02/23/online-video-content-in-search-for-benchmarks/. BENCHMARKS

9. Dan Ackerman Greenberg, "The Secret Strategies Behind Many 'Viral' Videos," November 22, 2007, TechCrunch.com. http://techcrunch.com/2007/11/22/the-secret-strategies-behind-many-viral-videos/.

10. Kevin Nalty, "Dear Stupid Marketer & Your Clueless Agency," November 27, 2007, http://willvideoforfood.com/2007/11/27/dear-stupid-marketer-and-your-clueless-agency/. STUPID

11. Christopher Lynn, "Please Standby: Rethinking Online Video Strategy," November 28, 2007, http://socialtnt.com/2007/11/28/please-standby-rethinking-online-video-strategy/. RETHINK

12. Kevin Nalty, "Farting in Public," March 27, 2007, www.youtube.com/watch?v=O3ejlkzDCuc. FART

13. Kevin Nalty, "Scary Maze," June 27, 2008, www.youtube.com/watch?v=W2R9YTXJeWE. SCARY

14. Kevin Nalty, "Sarah Palin Exposed," August 30, 2008, www.youtube.com/watch?v=v59mXowK2t8. PALIN

15. Venetian Princess (Jodie) YouTube Channel Page, www.youtube.com/venetianprincess. VENETIANPRINCESS

CHAPTER 4

1. Daniel Sevitt, "The Three Types of Online Video for Business," ReelSEO, November 26, 2009, www.reelseo.com/types-online-video-business/. 3TYPES

CHAPTER 5

1. Pew Internet & American Life Project, "Your Other Tube: Audience for Video-Sharing Sites Sources," July 29, 2009, http://pewresearch.org/pubs/1294/online-video-sharing-sites-use. PEW
2. Ibid.
3. Lawrence J. Najjar, "Multimedia Information and Learning," School of Psychology, Georgia Institute of Technology, 1996, http://citeseerx.ist.psu.edu/viewdoc/download. LEARNING
4. Gavin O'Malley, "Everybody Likes to Watch," Online Media Daily, July 29, 2009, www.mediapost.com/publications/?fa=Articles.showArticle&art_aid=110640. WATCH

CHAPTER 6

1. YouTube.com Fact Sheet: Demographic Information, www.youtube.com/t/fact_sheet. YOUTUBEFACTS

CHAPTER 7

1. "Emcees Jake and Amir," Digital Content Newfront, http://blip.tv/file/2109754/. GENERITECH

CHAPTER 8

1. Wikipedia Entry for Fred Figglehorn, http://en.wikipedia.org/wiki/Fred_Figglehorn. FREDWIKI

CHAPTER 11

1. Laurie Sullivan, "Google Tests Skipable Ads in YouTube Videos," MediaPost, September 11, 2009, www

.mediapost.com/publications/?fa=articles.showarticle& art_aid=117200. SKIPADS

2. Mike Shields, "Hulu's Ad Selector Could Set Web Video Pace," Media Week, February 4, 2010, www .adweek.com/aw/content_display/news/digital/e3i9f46c 57380aa314fa53f2eeef8a3ad4e. SELECTAD

CHAPTER 12

1. Google Trends, www.google.com/trends
2. Heather Dougherty, "Search and Social Networks Neck and Neck for Video Referrals," April 18, 2008 http://weblogs.hitwise.com/heather-dougherty/ 2008/04/post.html. SEMVIDEO
3. Amit Paunikar, "Calling Video Publishers," Google Video Blog, January 20, 2009, http://googlevideo .blogspot.com/2009/01/calling-video-publishers.html. GOOGLEVIDEO
4. comScore, "ComScore Releases March 2010 U.S. Search Engine Rankings" (press release), www .comscore.com/Press_Events/Press_Releases/2010/4/ comScore_Releases_March_2010_U.S._Search_Engine_ Rankings. YOUTUBESEARCH

Index

Account teams, 115
Ad networks, 12
Ad Selector, 159
Ad-safe content, 38
Advertisements
  branding beyond, 8
  call to action in, 65
  clever, 20–21
  costs of, 39
  dependence on, 265–266
  gag, 110–111
  growth of, 15–18
  irrelevant, 265
  location of, 23
  paid, 145–153
  passive-viewing states and, 86
  pop-up, 11–12
  pre-roll, 158–159
  scale of, 39
  social media, 86–87
  text, 37–38
  webstars *versus*, 135–136
  on YouTube, 10–11, 63–64
  YouTube revenue from, 96–97
Advertising agencies
  account leaders, 113–114
  brand strategy and, 113–115
  brands use of, 105–106
  case study, 111–113
  evolution of, 265
  external specialists for, 108–111
  image control and, 115–117
  innovation teams at, 107
  Internet knowledge, 106–107
  marketing without, 218
  power in, 106
  senior advocates at, 107
  social media engagement by,
    106–111
  videos creators and, 118–119
  webstars and, 110, 134–135, 141

Advisors, 6–7
Agencies. *See* Advertising agencies
Agency of record, 113–114
Algorithms, 97–98
Alka-Seltzer Great American Road
    Trip, 234–237
Amazon, 99
American Idol, 140, 255
Animal Lifeline, 219–220
Annotation text, 63–64
"Annoying Orange", 255–257
AnnoyingOrange, 35–36
"Ask A Ninja", 250
Audiences. *See also* Consumers
  attention spans of, 25–27
  continually building of, 231–232
  fragmentation of, 2
  for hidden content, 36–37
  meet ups organized by, 80
  Pew study of, 87
  segmentation of, 41–42
  URL, 67
  webstars' appeal to, 35–36
  YouTube's, characterization of,
    92–93
Autoplay, 72
"Auto Tune the News", 229–230
Awareness and intent surveys, 158

Back to the Future, 262
"Banana Man", 84
Banded entertainment, 13
Banners, 137
Barely Digital, 227–228
Barely Political, 226–228, 232
Beatles, 123
Beebe, J. D., 221
Benson, Greg, 83, 240–243
Berg, Ilsa, 212
Best of breed approach, 114–115
"Best Commercials video, 68

Bieber, Justin, 230–231
BigJoeSmith, 197
Black20, 213
BlogPluse, 221–222
Blogs, lifespan of, 88
Boedigheimer, Dane, 35, 254–257
Boyle, Susan, 53–54
Brand channels, 149
Branded entertainment
   changing content of, 131
   characterization of, 119–120
   history of, 13
   measuring, 161–162
   product placement and, 21
Brands
   advertising augmentation by, 131
   agencies serving, 105–106
   agency strategies for, 113–115
   awareness of, 76
   conservative, 24
   creating, 199–200
   entertainment value of, 5–6
   image control and, 115–117
   ROI prospect criteria, 156–157
   stars links to, 3
   webstars and, 133–134, 139–143
Break Media, 214
Britain's Got Talent, 53
Buckley, Michael, 250
   style of, 199
   videos by, viewers, 168–169
Bud.tv, 5
Budweiser, 5–6
Burn Notice, 212
Business exchangers, 156
Business videos. *See also* Business
   videos; Conversion videos;
   Educational videos; Viral videos
   advantages of, 218
   considerations for, 76–77
   content use by, 15
   corporate communication and,
      77–78
   custom, benefits of, 76–77
   framework for, 76
   on site posting of, 76
   types of, 68

Businesses. *See also* Startups
   Internet relations of, 115–117
   revenue share, 157
Butler, Shay
   about, 257–259
   feedback from, 178
   interview with, 258–260
   "tard" children video by, 54

Call to action, 65–67
Campaigns
   Hitview, 136–138
   home-page videos, 148–149
   integrated, 150
   multi-level marketing, 156
   pay to play, 147
   URLs, 66
   value of, determining, 157–158
   Vaseline example, 17–18
   webstars and, 132
Carl's Jr., 140, 244
Casino, 252
"Charlie Bit My Finger", 54–55
Chaplin, Charlie, 123
Chicago Tribune, 251
Clothing retailers, 156–157
CMP. *See* Cost per impression (CPM)
Coke, 8, 87
   American Idol and, 136, 140
   "happy vending machine" by, 51
   pre-roll ads by, 159
   video content with, 159
Coke-Mentos Fountain, 116–117
Colbert, Stephen, 168
Collabs
   definition of, 180
   etiquette of, 187–191
   personal experiences with, 81–83
Community
   acceptance by, 210
   discovery of, 79–80
   engaging with, 219
   growth of, 18
   opportunities from, 199
   participants, 80–81
   passion for, 81–82
   physical, 83–84

revenues, 109, 206–207
segmentation of, 42
understanding of, 183–185
violations of, 178
webstars and, 41, 142
ComScore, 2, 16
Conservative organizations, 24
Consumers. *See also* Audiences
brand awareness of, 5, 25
changing preferences, 105–106
contests and, 24
engaging, 47
Google searches by, 60–62
irritation of, 47
purchasing behavior of, 47–48
video watching habits of, 4
videos generated by, 13
Content. *See also* Professional
content
audience segmentation and, 41–42
digital studio generated, 33–35
hidden, 32–33, 36–39
hyper niche, 36
monetary value-based, 33
most popular, 51–58
niches, filling, 207–208
professional, 13–15, 32
professionally produced, 263–264
text, importance of, 168
user-generated, 31–32
Contests
creators of, 21
fear of, 24
sponsoring, 47
Conversion videos
advantages of, 71
creation of, 71–72
success metrics for, 72–73
Coors, 244
Copyright infringements, 198
Corporate communications, 77–78
Cost per impression (CPM)
ads based on, 145–146
banners, 137–138
definition of, 7
guarantees for, 11
limits of, 8

measuring, 161–162
premium charges for, 39
studies of, 158
Costs. *See also* Monetization
advertisement, 39
hidden content, 39
production, 22–23
ROI and, 22–23
viral video, 46–47
Coulter, Ann, 228
Coupons, 66
Cousin Brucie, 123
Cowell, Simon, 180
Crocker, Chris, 50
Cruikshank, Lucas, 35, 124
Curry, Adam, 123
Cyrus, Miley, 57

Damage control, 77–78
Dancing, on viral videos, 53
"DaneBoe", 35, 254–258
Day, Felicia, 35
DeFranco, Phil, 168–169
DFTBA Records, 247, 250
Digital incubation model, 214
Digital studios, 33–35
Direct response
abusing, 196–197
campaigns, 155–156
metrics for, 22
Discovery network, 127–129
Disney-ABC, 212, 215, 260
Dissintermediate, 77
Do it yourself (DYI) content, 57–58
Domino's, 77
Donnelly, Michael, 116
Donovan, Lisa, 125, 250
Dr. Ruth, 123
"Doctor Horrible's Sing-Along Blog",
34–35

Ecosystems, 8–9
EdBassmaster, 53
Editors, 97–98, 197
Educational videos
advantages of, 74
function of, 73–74
success metrics for, 75

EepyBird, 116–117
"Electric Spoofaloo", 211
Electric Farm, 214
Electric Farm Entertainment, 214
"Elf Yourself", 49
eMarketer, 16
Entertainment. *See also* Branded
    entertainment
  demand for, 3
  flops, 5
  focus on, 25, 27
  information *versus*, 265–266
  persuasive forms of, 8
  product placement, 21
Entrepreneurs. *See* Businesses;
    Startups
Ettinger, Amber, 227
Evergreen, 58
Evey, Kim, 241–242
Evian, 10, 44
Evian Roller Babies, 44
"Evolution of Dance", 53

Facebook
  advertising on, 86–87
  function of, 86
  performance data from, 84
"Failblog", 56
Fail, 55–56
"Farting in Public"
  inspiration for, 53
  popularity of, 199–200
  tags to, 99
Fey, Tina, 56
Fiesta project, 252
Film Riot, 161–162
Ford Motor Company, 252
Fox Broadcasting, 122
Fox Digital Media, 213
Fox Television Studios, 211–212
Fox, Michael J., 262
"Fox 15 Gigs", 211–212, 214
Friedman, Brent, 214
Friendships, parasocial, 37
Fulgoni, Gian, 16

GagFilms, 35–36
Gambito, Christine, 82, 220
Garfield, Steve, 201, 244–247

General Electric, 150
Generation ADHD, 25–27
"Generi-Tech", 120
*Get Seen: Online Video Secrets to
    Building Your Business*,
    244–245
"G-Force", 215
Gigs, 213
Gizmodo, 193
GoDaddy bosom thumbnail, 169
Godin, Seth, 45
Good Morning America, 243
Google, 196
  alerts, 220
  customer searches of, 60–62
  forms used by, 163
  pre-roll ads on, 158–159
  proprietary scheme of, 101
  revenue, 96–97
  successful approaches to, 166–172
  text advertisements, 37–38
  trend tracking on, 221
  unsuccessful approaches to,
    170–171
  video creation help from, 223
  video index, 171–173
  YouTube and, 98–103, 165–166,
    174
Google Bombing, 168
GooTube Conspiracy, 201
Gore, Al, 46
"Gorgeous Tiny Chicken Machine
    Show", 240, 242
Green, Hank, 247–249
Greenberg, Dan Ackerman, 51
The Gregory Brothers, 229–230
"Greg Hits Hollywood", 241, 243
Gross rating points (GRPs), 7
"The Guild", 240–241
"Guy Catches Glasses with Face", 244

"HaHaHa", 54
Hallerman, David, 15
"Happy Vending Machine", 51
HappySlip, 82
  collaboration with, 185, 188
  humanizing activities of, 220
  style of, 199–200

Harris, Neil Patrick Harris, 34
HBO Labs, 125–126
"Healthymagination", 64, 150
Hidden content
　ad-safe, 38
　audiences for, 36–37
　cost factors of, 39
　description of, 32–33
　quality, 37
　relevance of, 37–38
Hill, Caitlin, 122–123
Hitviews
　clients of, 135–136
　costs of, 136–137, 162
　founding of, 122–123
　guarantees by, 133
　stars on, 137–138, 162
Holding companies, 115
Home-page videos
　aggressive campaigns of, 148–149
　avoidance of, 146–147
　takeovers, 99–100
Honors, 181, 189
"Hooking Up", 83, 126, 253
How-to videos, 222–223
Howcast, 57–58, 150
"How to Become Popular on
　YouTube Without Any Talent",
　177–178, 188
Hulu
　audience for, 2
　pre-roll ads on, 159
　professional content on, 263–264
　search engines and, 173–174
　TV linked to, 262
Humor, 54–55
Hyper niche content, 36
Hyperlinks, 65–66

IAB. *See* Interactive Advertising
　Bureau (IAB)
IAB standards, 160
"I Got a Crush on Obama", 227, 232
Impressions, 7–8
In-stream ads. *See* Pre-rolls
Inbound links, 168
"Internet Killed Television", 253
Interactive Advertising Bureau (IAB)

　function of, 152
　pre-roll report by, 158
　standers, 160
Interactive agency, 114
Internet, 4, 110
　access to, 48
　ads on, 37, 105–106, 136
　agencies knowledge of, 106–107
　agency use by, 105, 114
　audience for, 27
　brands and, 13, 113, 116
　business understanding of, 93, 115
　ComScore of, 16
　corporate images and, 115–117
　location, 23
　percentage of users, 84–85, 87
　short-form videos on, 200
　viral videos on, 69–70
Internetainers, 234
InVideo ad, 64
"I've Got a Crush on Obama", 55
"I Want My Three Minutes Back", 125

JeepersMedia, 103
JetBlue, 77
"Jews Need to Be Perfected", 228

Karbasfrooshan, Ashkan, 33
Kelly, Devon, 211
Keywords
　bloating of, 195–196
　searches, 21–22
　subscribing to, 94
Kimmel, Jimmy, 136, 161
Koyaanisqatsi, 151

Lady Gaga, 57
Lane, Nathan, 123
Lastufka, Alan, 249–252
"Lay Me Off", 47
"Leave Britney Alone", 50
Lie to Me, 137
Link bait, 169
Link, Neal, 234
LisaNova, 125, 195, 250
Lohan, Lindsay, 36
LonelyGirl15, 230
Lucas, Fred, 125

MacBook Air, 192–193
Machinima.com, 257–258
Mainstream culture, 228–232
Marano, Gabriel, 212–214
Market mixing, 25
Marketers
  customer pursuit by, 84
  on-line knowledge needs of, 4–9
  patience of, 25–26
  social media's importance to, 89
  video promotion by, 264
  webstar communication with,
    134–135
  YouTube knowledge and, 91–95
Marketing. *See also* Online videos
  funnel, 59–60
  public relations *versus*, 117–118
  purple cow, 45–46
  push, 45
  rules of, 4
  social media and, 89
  viewers' attention spans and,
    25–27
Mathieu, Michael, 17
The Maury Povich Show, 243
McLaughlin, Rhett, 234
Media agency, 114
Media RSS feeds, 171–173
MediocreFilms, 241
Medium experts, 115
Mentos, 116–117, 142
Metacafe, 98
Microbilt, 237
The Middle Show, 213
Monetization, 206–210
Morrow, Bruce, 123
Most-subscribed videos
  characterization of, 13, 122
  content of, 40, 94–95
  vloggs 57
  webstar promotion of, 13–14, 188
MrSafety, 189–190
MTV Video, 123, 214
Multi-level marketing campaigns, 156
Music videos
  parodies, 56–57
  viewers of, 53–54

"My Box in a Box", 226

"Nalts", 170
  CNN coverage of, 56
  debut of, 54
  posting on, 190
Netflix, 161–162
"The New Anti-Social: Free Ways to
    Track and Trend Online", 221
Newsweek, 227
Next New Networks, 227–230, 232
Numa Numa, 28

"Obama Girl"
  conception of, 218
  media response to, 227
  mythology behind, 231
  popularity of, 51–52
  timing of, 228–229
Obama, Barack, 110, 228
Of Mice and Men (Steinbeck), 25
"The Onion", 37
Online videos. *See also* Business
    videos
  ads surrounding, 11–12
  advantages of, teaching, 160
  branded approach to, 111–113
  community of, 18–19, 79–83
  content layers, 32–33
  contests and, 21
  cost per view, 136–138
  creating, rules for, 3–4
  creators of, 118–119
  cultural infusion of, 228–232
  currency of, 170
  definition of, 1–2
  descriptions of, 167
  engagement on, 169
  evolution of, 9–18
  future of, 262–263
  growth of, 24–25
  home-page, 146–147
  iconic, 226
  inbound links for, 168
  investors for, 206
  key aspects of, 4–9
  keyword searches and, 21–22

mainstreaming, 225–226
maturation of, 233
monetization of, 206–208
mythology surrounding, 230–231
next big thing, 266
packaging of, 202–203
play time and, 200–201
popular, 19–20
production costs of, 22–23
production quality of, 200–201
quality of, 19–20
seeding, 191–193
social media *versus*, 84–89
stars of. *See* Webstars
studios creation of, 210–215
style of, 198–200
timing of, 168–169
titles, 167
TV viewers and, 263–264
uniqueness, 229–230
uploading, 166
web site content and, 167
"Opportunities in Online Video", 26
Organizations. *See* Brands

Paid advertising
brand channels, 149
critique of, 151–153
future of, 150
home-page videos, 146–149
integrated campaigns, 150
partner program, 147–148
penny ads, 145–146
proven models for, 145
Palin, Sarah, 55–56
Parasocial friendships, 37
Parodies, 56–57, 120
Participatory web series, 215
Partner program
advantage of, 101
debut of, 148
major advertisers in, 147–148
members of, 122
professionals on, 39–40
revenues from, 13, 181, 209
stars on, 35
webstar case study, 127–129

Pay-per-view, 10–11
"Pay to play" campaigns, 147
"Penguin Army", 46
Penny ads, 145–146
"Penny Pranks", 49–50
Pepsi, 116
"Perfect Pour", 244
Performance data, 84
Perry, Katy, 57
Physical community, 83–84
Pirillo, Chris, 201
PlaceVine, 156
Play time, 200–201
Political humor, 54–55
Pollak, Kevin, 252
Pop-up advertisements, 11–12
PopTub, 101
Potter, Chuck, 125
Pranked, 53
Pranks, 53
Pre-rolls, 16, 158–160
Proctor & Gamble, 13
Production quality, 200–201
Professional content
characterization of, 32
growth of, 13–15
webstars *versus*, 263–264
"Project for Awesome", 248
Promoted videos, 147
Public relations, 114, 117–118
Purple Cow, 45–46
Push marketing, 45

Quarterlife, 211

Ray-Ban, 244
Reagan, Ronald, 78
Real time indexing, 86
Relles, Ben, 51–52, 218, 232
Renetto, 82–83, 188–190
Response. *See* Direct response
"The Retarded Policeman", 83,
240
"Rethinking the Digital Studio",
210–215
Return on investment (ROI)
brand-specific models, 155–157

Return on investment (*Continued*)
  branded entertainment, 161–162
  impact *versus* reach and, 157–158
  measurements of, 7
  online video, 6
  pre-rolls, 158–160
  production costs and, 22–23
Revenue share entrepreneur, 156
Revenues. *See* Monetization
Rhett and Link, 234–237
Richman, Keith, 214
Ries, Al, 48
Rivera, Jodie, 237–240
Robertson, Mark, 163
Robot blogs, 171
ROI. *See* Return on investment (ROI)

Sabo, Walter, 122–123
Samsung, 230
ScanScout, 17
"Scary Maze", 49, 53
"Scary Hitchhiker Prank", 53
Search engine marketing (SEM), 164
Search engine optimization (SEO),
  164, 167
Search engines. *See also specific types*
  impact of, 163
  keywords and, 21–22
  market sustainability of, 205–206
  marketing with, 164–165
  optimization of, 220
  real time indexing by, 86
  weaknesses of, 173–175
  YouTube and, 84, 93–94
Seeding, 10, 191–193
Self-promotion, 194
SEM. *See* Search engine marketing
  (SEM)
SEO. *See* Search engine optimization
  (SEO)
7Echo, 150
"7 Things Guys Don't Have To Do",
  238
"ShayCarl", 258
"Shaytards", 258
Sherpa. *See* Advisors
Site maps, 171–173

60 Frames, 212
Slater, Brett, 210
Smirnoff, 46–47
Smosh, 189, 199
Social media
  marketing with, 89
  niche specialists, 108–111
  online video *versus*, 84–89
  start-up specialists, 108–111
Social media monitoring, 220–222
Spam, 171
Spamming, 194–195
Spears, Britney, 57
Speed, Alli, 253
Spiders, 172, 175
Spotlight videos
  partners' program and, 198
  pay-to-play and, 147
  selection of, 97
Stage 9, 212
Stars. *See* Webstars
Startups
  amateur talent for, 218
  how-to videos and, 222–223
  humanizing, 219–220
  search engine use by, 219–220
  social-media monitoring by,
    220–222
  video distributions services
    for, 222
  webstars for, 218–219
"The Station", 258
Studios, 210–215
Subscribers. *See also*
  Most-subscribed videos
  attracting, 103, 128, 131–132
  definition of, 180
  interaction among, 80
  to keywords, 94, 224
  leech, 187
  quality of, 188–189
  social ladder based on, 184–185
  titles and, 202–203
  vlogging, 57
  webstars and, 13–14, 21
  YouTube, 132
Surveys, 158

T-Pain, 230
T180 studios, 211
Take 180 studios, 214–215, 260
"Tea Partay", 46–47
Technorati Tracking, 222
Television
    advertisements on, 12
    cable, 207
    online videos on, 262–264
    product pitches on, 264
    promotion on, 67
    time-shifted, 45
Text advertisements, 37–38
"The Guild", 35
TheHill88, 123
TheStation, 188
3/4 rule, 186
Thumbnails
    definition of, 165
    function of, 165, 171–173
    inappropriate, 171
    selection of, 202
Titles
    optimizing searches with, 167
    role of, 172, 202–203
Tootsie, 55
Trend Search, 221–222
Trendrr.com, 221
Trippy, Charles, 252–253
Trolling, 171
Trout, Jack, 48
"Truth of Fail", 248
TubeMogul, 9, 133
Turd dropping, 186
Twitter, 86–88

URLs
    campaign, 66
    in description, 65
    qualified viewers for, 67
USA Network, 212
User-generated content (UGC), 31
The Usual Suspects, 252

Valemont, 214
Vaseline campaign, 17–18
"VenetianPrincess", 56–57, 237–238

Video companion ad, 146
Video distributions services, 222
Video Volunteers, 248
Viewers. *See* Audiences
"The Viralest Video", 226–227
"Viral Video Chart", 50–51
Viral videos
    characterization of, 69–70
    children in, 54–55
    commonalties of, 51–58
    conversion rates of, 22
    dancing on, 53
    death of, 43–45
    definition of, 48–49
    down market appeal of, 49–50
    duration of, 51
    evolution of, 10
    fails on, 55–56
    how to, 57–58
    laws of, 48–51
    limitations of, 45–48
    manipulation and, 51
    music on, 53–54, 56–57
    political humor on, 54–55
    pranks on, 53
    proliferation of, 27–29
    quality of, 49
    success metrics for, 70
    topical nature of, 50
    uniqueness of, 50–51
    vlogging on, 57
Vlogging, 57

Washington Post, 227
WatchMojo, 33
Webstars. *See also* YouTube
        popularity; *individual stars*
    ad campaigns and, 132
    agencies teaming with, 110
    audience appeal of, 35–36
    brands use by, 139–143
    case study, 127–129
    characteristics of, 12–13, 131
    communication with, 134–135
    community of, 41, 142
    compensation for, 219
    contacting, 218–219

Webstars (*Continued*)
  conventional myth about, 125–127
  CPM of, 137–138
  creation of, 121–124
  endorsement by, 135–136
  fans of, 131–133, 169
  Hitviews campaigns, 136–138
  impact model of, 138–139
  linking brands to, 3
  most viewed, 253
  on partner program, 39–40
  promotion by, 19, 133–134
  talents of, 126–127
Weinstein, Bob, 122
WhatTheBuckShow, 199, 250
When Ninjas Attack, 212
Whitney, Daisy, 210–211
"Who Wants to Be an Internet
  Millionaire", 253
Wikipedia, 116
Williams, Chris M., 211, 215
Winfrey, Oprah, 124, 127
Wipe-Out, 212
Wright, Reverend Jeremiah, 228–229

"You Such at Photoshop", 37
"YouTube Etiquette", 186–187
YouTube, 23, 234. *See also* Partner
  program; Subscribers
  account creation, 93
  advertisements on, 10–11,
    146–147
  advertising revenue, 208
  algorithms, 97–98
  audience of, 92–93
  basics, 91–93
  brand channels, 149
  chain reactions on, 98
  collaborative video development
    by, 81–83
  community. *See* Community
  damage control via, 77
  Discovery network and, 127–129
  dominance of, 2
  driving traffic via, 62–69
  editors' role, 97–98
  featured videos, 97

gatherings, 83–84
Google and, 98–103, 165–166,
  174
HBO series, 83
hyperlinks on, 65–66
identity content, 94–95
launch of, 10
monetization and, 208–210
monitoring service, 94
most videos on, 28–29
most viewed star on, 253
origins of, 87
ownership of, 196
paid approaches to, 63–65
professional content on, 39–40,
  263–264
revenues, 13, 96–97
sales representatives, 111
searches on, 93–94, 173–174
social media *versus*, 84–89
stars on, 12–13
tips for, 102–103
TV linked to, 262
user base, 92
video posting on, 99–100
viewers, attracting, 95–96
YouTube popularity. *See also*
  Webstars
  advantages of, 182–183
  creative style and, 198–200
  disadvantages of, 181–182
  etiquette and, 186–191
  interaction and, 190
  negativity and, 197–198
  overview, 177–180
  packaging and, 202–203
  persistence and, 190
  play time and, 200–201
  posting frequency and, 191
  production quality and, 201–202
  quality and, 189
  short-term boost for, 193–197
  social media vehicles and, 191–193
  summary, 203–204
*YouTube: An Insider's Guide to
  Climbing the Charts*, 250
YuMe, 16–17

More experts in the New Rules of Social Media series...